T0380344

WEAVING LIFE

My magic carpet ride through the world of rugs presented by Rugology World™

CYNTHIA "SALONISTA" KOSCIUCZYK

© 2021 Cynthia "Salonista" Kosciuczyk. All rights reserved.

No part of this book may be reproduced, stored in a retrieval system, or transmitted by any means without the written permission of the author.

AuthorHouse™
1663 Liberty Drive
Bloomington, IN 47403
www.authorhouse.com
Phone: 833-262-8899

Because of the dynamic nature of the Internet, any web addresses or links contained in this book may have changed since publication and may no longer be valid. The views expressed in this work are solely those of the author and do not necessarily reflect the views of the publisher, and the publisher hereby disclaims any responsibility for them.

This book is printed on acid-free paper.

ISBN: 978-1-6655-4987-5 (hc)
ISBN: 978-1-6655-1707-2 (sc)
ISBN: 978-1-6655-1708-9 (e)

Library of Congress Control Number: 2021903281

Print information available on the last page.

Published by AuthorHouse 02/23/2022

CONTENTS

"International in scope and in flavor, Weaving Life blends historical accuracy with poetic intimacy. Ideal for the dyed-in-the-wool rug lover."

-Best-selling author and entrepreneur Damon Brown (www.damonbrown.net)

What's my rug? In this fun and deeply personal tribute to the art and history of Oriental rugs, *Weaving Life* is part encyclopedia, part soul-baring journey, and part ode to the rich cultural tradition of handmade rugs. It is entwined with beautiful poetry and anecdotes from more than twenty years of working in the rug industry and living and traveling overseas. Cynthia Kosciuczyk has written lovingly of her passion for rugs, the unspoken dialect of symbols, colors, and threads of the world.

--Taylor Baldwin Kiland, author of *Lessons from the Hanoi Hilton: Six Characteristics of High-Performance Teams*

"We travel long distances, we puzzle over the meaning of a painting or a book, but what we are wanting to see, we are that." - Rumi

DEDICATION

To the Persian community of San Diego, I thank you. A special mention to PEYK magazine who gave me the wonderful privilege of publishing a few of them over 10 years ago. To the Jodari family who gave me the gift of rug history and legends. To those who encouraged my love of rugs and sharing that knowledge: Barry O'Connell, Dusty Roberts, Paul Lucas, Scott Waring. Those who were so helpful sharing your information and passion: The Mikaeli family, Richard Inman, the Prospect Rug Gallery, Nia Pirnia. To some of the people I met because of rugs like Salar, Renaissance Rugs, Harout Torkomian, and Art Resources, I thank you for understanding my quest for knowledge. To those who have let me share my stories: Cam Mayville, Brian Jesperson, Doug Heifferman, and Dave Randolph. I am grateful for the opportunity! Adding color to my knowledge, Chris Howell, and Issa Hoker. Special thanks to Adi Pourfard of Aja Rugs who so generously gave their time and help.

A very big thank you to Koren's Metro Flooring for appreciating my background and keeping me in the fibers! So, let's begin, I touched a thread, and the story of Weaving Life began.

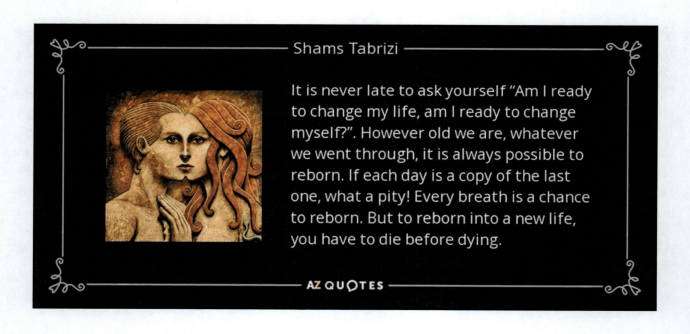

Shams Tabrizi

It is never late to ask yourself "Am I ready to change my life, am I ready to change myself?". However old we are, whatever we went through, it is always possible to reborn. If each day is a copy of the last one, what a pity! Every breath is a chance to reborn. But to reborn into a new life, you have to die before dying.

AZ QUOTES

CHAPTER 1

HISTORY

The first rug I ever knew, my grandmother's painted Sarouk, inspired my soul and fed my imagination. Having no idea what a wonderful work of art lay on the floor, I traced the patterns with my tiny hands. Now with experience, I realize what a treasure we gave our cousin when we divided grandmother's estate.

Remembering my first impressions of rugs as an adult began when I got married and began living Athens in 1988, our monthly excursions to the Oracle of Delphi, to see the foliage, feel the mystical connections, and purchase the wooly cream colored flokatis. The Turkish kilims and deep black goat's hair rugs that we were gifted by family and gave me a sense of mystery.

The Greek factory in Piraeus where I worked dyeing textiles had woven silk in the olden days as finely as I weave this story. My search for understanding woven fibers began with my fascination with their culture, history, art and even religion wrapped within.

When I arrived in the Gaslamp of San Diego, after 12 years overseas, I looked for places reminiscent of my ancient home. I walked into the 4th Avenue Rug Gallery. Falling in love with an octagon rug in the window, I crossed the threshold to another space and time. A world of rugs! The owners were from Tabriz, my eyes lit up as in the Rubaiyat's of Rumi, Shamus-i-Tabriz, I knew in my soul there was something to learn here.

Over twenty years in the industry I have met wholesalers, retailers, repairmen, cleaners and rug lovers and world travelers. Growing my knowledge base year after year, knot by knot, their story drew me in deeper. I studied many threads of education that made me love them even more! To rug friends, collectors and business owners who shared their stories with me, and all the chat rooms revolving around rugs and textiles, I love you!

Their story started me crafting poems to describe my experiences with rugs as my only company. The thing I realized is that rugs hold a woven memory for me in my mind's eye. I remember textiles as if they were my creations or my very own children. With this deep passion for the woven textiles, the symbols and stories they contain, the people that are the process from fiber to rug, I give you the work of my heart: Weaving Life.

CHAPTER 2

RUG LOVERS

Rug Lovers

They came from far and wide

Lovers of the thread!

Share a story, learn a Skill.

They filled the room with color: yellow, blue and red.

The masters and the new

United together for a shared view.

Rugs tell tales from the old Silk Road to New South Wales

Love rugs and know you are not alone.

Textiles will take you as far as you will go!

Rug Lover is a term that describes all of us with a passion for the woven textiles!

Such a special soul loves rug. The term describes one whose devotion and admiration to the field is best described as "love". Considering the way that almost every word or story that lights up my eyes is about rugs, so I believe it was destiny that bought me to this group of others of my kind! Years ago, I got introduced to a group online Rug Lovers and website, Spongo Bongo (Strange name, wonderful data!). I had gone to an exhibition about a Yurt that was brought to San Diego. Oct 12, 2008 - Aug 1, 2009. Highlights included recent gifts to the Museum—a prize-winning Kyrgyz yurt, beautiful Persian bag faces and Central Asian hats.

The magnificent yurt, a round, domed, trellis-tent dwelling, 22 feet in diameter, won first prize in a national contest, celebrating the 1000th anniversary of the Kyrgyz epic Manas. Five years in design and construction, it boasts patterned screens, made of thin reed stems wrapped in colored wool, used for covering the latticed walls of the structure, as well as for room dividers. Felted wool, a Kyrgyz specialty, is seen in the yurt's intricately patterned, colorful rugs.

The yurt, which was brought to the United States by Christy Walton, was originally shown at the Museum's Balboa Park location in 1997 in the exhibition _*YURTA—A Central Asian Nomad's Hearth and Home*_ . Walton, a sponsor of both exhibitions, donated the yurt to the Museum in 2007.

Journeying from Kyrgyzstan to erect the large tent in the Museum's ground floor Grand Plaza Gallery were Mekenbek Osmonaliyev, who with his mother designed and built the yurt, and brothers Ishembi and Raiymbek Obolbekov. As part of the installation process, the tent was put up and taken down several times between October 2 and 11 to film the process in detail. Visitors were able watch this fascinating procedure. On view were rare Kyrgyz reed screens and stunning Turkoman, Uzbek and Kazakh costumes and textiles on loan from several private collections in Southern California as well as from the Museum's permanent collection.

Dr. Sussana Babaie, visiting scholar at the Getty Research Institute and an authority on Islamic art and architecture, presented a lecture "Persianate Traditions the City and the Meadow" on November 1, 2008. A workshop, "Inspired Felting," took place on November 8, 2008. On December 13, 2008 a Persian Family Festival took place that included traditional music and dance and calligraphy demonstrations. "The Yurt—Ancient Dwelling, Modern Lifestyle" was the subject of a lecture by Alan Bair, owner and president of Pacific Yurts, Inc. on January 10, 2009 and Sights and Sounds of the Silk Road, a program of music, dance, and folk tales, was presented by The Silk Road Music and Dance Ensemble on February 14, 2009. This interaction got me delving deeply into writing about textiles. It was like a brave new world for me.

I had been planning a few days off to join in a workshop at the New School of Architecture! **On Friday Sept. 11th, 2009, 120 artists, architects, designers, and community members gathered at the New School of Architecture to participate in a design charette on affordable housing for artists. These participants were broken up into 16 groups. After being briefed on the nine prototypical sites each group chose one to work on. Groups were given guidelines pertaining to the desired outcome of the charette, which was to "determine goals, as they relate to the potential for affordable artist live/work units and related spaces, for each site." These groups developed land-use options, produced sketches, and discussed the concepts for artist affordable housing on the site they had chosen. There was also a lot of discussion on community connectivity and building 'green'. The result of this process was lots of interesting and innovative ideas, sketches, notes, and designs, which were displayed on the walls around at the end of the night. I had taken a few days and was able to answer the call. "Will you teach rug ID in Las Vegas? Yes, Absolutely! The decision to attend was life changing! Everyone who was anyone in rugs, cleaning, appraisals, and repairs attended! Even Howard Partridge and HALI were there! This year someone reminded me of that trip!**

Once I finally got to manuscript, I shared it with many rug loving friends. One of my favorite rug mentors, Richard Inman asked what about finding the reasons why others got involved in the industry? I had an online radio show years ago and love impromptu interviews. Thus, this next session is just that.

Most of the folks I asked I collaborate regularly with, so the conversation flowed. One rug dealer who is of the upper echelons of collecting asked not to be included as he felt that modern rugs have evolved into soulless floor coverings, losing some of their authentic nomadic spirit and unique voice. Compared to a nomadic tribal wonder, a flawlessly executed pattern can seem from another world all together! I had brief interviews with my colleagues in the business. I tried to capture the essence of the industry!

1.   What is their favorite rug and why?

2.   How did the end up in the Oriental Rug Business?

3.   What is the lesson they have learned?

These are written in the order I had a conversation!

Chris Howell (Dye Specialist and Educator) Washington D.C. loves the Persian Silk Qum that reflects the passion of the weaver's exquisite art! Afghani Kazaks for the vivid colors: Monaco blue, green, yellow. He got started with his cleaning business in Washington DC and because of a dog accident he began working in handmade rugs. Why does he love them? Each handmade textile is a piece of art created with passion and shares the weavers' story. In the way that music is the language of emotion, rugs help you to see the picture"

Nia Pirnia (Flooring Services Inc.) CA

Loves Bijars because of their multilevel beauty! His family was in the rug business in the wholesale business made sense to continue the legacy. Rug business is a complicated business for making money, yet because of the passion once you get involved it's not possible to get out. There is such a hierarchy of trade from the weavers, to the groups to the merchants to the bazaar to the shippers to the consumers.

Brian Jespersen (Artistic Rug Care) KS

Favorite rug is the Eagle Kazaks due to the intricate patterns and bold colors!

When he retired from the military, he got involved in the cleaning business. One of his wealthy clients begged him to clean his hand made rugs. One of them had a bad stain. He spoke to Interlink, and they referred him to Rug cleaning expert and soap guru, Paul Lucas. He found the solution and has been happy ever since. He says, "Never judge a rug by the way it looks. It could be an antique or have deep sentimental value. Textiles have an emotional component; you can never guess the stories that may be associated with it."

Barry O'Connell (World Renowned Rug Expert) PA

His most reassure rug is the Hamadan from the 1850's because its natural purple dye.

Politics is the reason he got involved in the rug world. He was very involved in the Political scene in Washington DC. In the 1980's one of the TV stations was covering a conference where Bud Dwyer committed suicide live during conference.

Barry decided that his hobby should be something much more esoteric and got involved in Oriental rugs and the Textile Museum.

He went on a tour with Ron O'Callaghan and became enamored with design/pattern/ Afghanistan. His best lesson from the rugs: Math is easy. Rugs are woven with the nonverbal language. For each dialect spoken, each region has its own woven language. The symmetry is in the knot count all wrapped in the selvages.

Paul Lucas (Chem Max® Corp.) MI

He loves the Moshwani Prayer Rugs because they have two different styles of knots: Persian and Senna. It's from NW Iran with a wool foundation, warp with a barber pole weave. He began as carpet cleaners refused to wash the handmade pieces. Had an Epiphany of how to clean them in the 1970's with Majid's carpets and began the journey with LST and Ed York, the rest is history! He says: "You are never done learning. You are cleaning art, not things. Rugs made him understand that's how they share ideas."

Shawn Bagheri (Prospect Rug Gallery) CA

His most treasured rug is Makhteshim Kashan's circa 1870-1900's true handmade art, he is also fond of Senna Heriz' from 1870-1920.He went to college in Germany at 21. The largest carpet store was in Munich. He met the manager Mr. Lipschitz and there began his journey working with the art they call rugs. His wisdom he has learned from the rugs: "All that one makes with such patience is divine art."

Fernanda Lay(Aja Rugs) CA

Her most special rug is the ones from Malayer because of the patterns and colors they incorporate and the quality of the wool. The patterns read like a book of different stories in their symmetry. After school for Interior design and worked at an architecture firm. She wasn't happy and walked into see a friend at Aja rugs. A year later Adi offered a job to help design some modern rugs and it became her passion.

She says: "So many amazing relationships because of the rugs."

Adi Pourfard (Aja Rugs) CA

Feels his favorite rug is Malayer (tribal rug) Tribal rugs are my favorite due to imperfection designs. How did he get there? I was always somewhat involved in the Rug Business. After school, it felt natural for me since I knew the business and enjoyed doing it. I learned that every person has a reason for life and mine is to be the voice of the weavers to bring the arts in to the market.

Dave Nichols (Rug Renew) CA

The rugs Josheghan call to him because of the colors deep dark blues, purples as each color has a meaning. He especially loves the rugs from Turkey the cobalt blue as its their color that expresses "happiness" Having done cleaning for world travelers and collectors, the whole idea called to him. He decided to get his training and dedicate his life to cleaning and care of this woven art. He shared" The rugs embrace a lifetime journey of learning".

Jason Mikaeli (Mikaeli Rug) CA

Family roots and favorite rugs are from Bijar because they are strongest Persian rug possible and have rich patterns. His grandfather was in the rug business 1963-1968 in 1982 they had a store in Denmark before they came to America. Why he loves rugs?

"Every day you learn something. There is so much love woven within."

Michael Rose (One World Rug Care) NM was by far one of the most fascinating conversations I had in the rug arena. His family roots and business brought him full circle to the rug business after a career as a Golf pro. One of the best parts in the conversation was when his father assigned him to read all the rug books in the shop collection and write a report! That time in deep study so contributed to his knowledge and expertise today.

Harriet Adams (ABC Oriental Carpet Cleaning) Ithaca NY Loves the carpets from Heriz because of the patterns and colors. Their cleaning business began in 1980's and they found the need for handmade rugs experts. They became involved in the education aspect as well. What inspires her is always learning more and sharing that knowledge with her customers.

Issa Hoker (The Rug Colorist) FLA Her most favorite rug is the first handwoven rug I purchased when I got into rug dyeing. It has a tribal feel with brightly colored patterns and braided fringes. In 2014, I relocated from Florida to California, and wanted to start a new business. After some market research, I decided to start a carpet cleaning business. I had no experience with carpets or rugs. After a couple of months of starting that business, I noticed carpets that were bleached and when I inquired about how to fix them, I was told the area would have to be "patched" or the whole carpet replaced. But it couldn't be. There had to be another option. And upon researching this carpet issue, I discovered a whole world of restoring carpets and rugs with dyes. I still remember when I saw a carpet being dyed on YouTube, my heartbeat faster, and I was hooked! I knew right then and there that I wanted to learn all I could about carpet and rug dyeing. So, I dropped everything else immersed myself in the carpet dyeing world. That's when The Rug Colorist was born. I like to say that Oriental rugs are much like people. They when faded, they can be restored, and the older they get, the more beautiful and valuable they become. The imperfections and irregularities become an integral part of its character and beauty. If one is looking for a perfect rug, they should purchase a machine-made rug. If one is looking for a beautiful and timeless rug, the hand-woven rug is they choice.

Cynthia Kosciuczyk (Designer Tastes) CA

I love Nain rugs, the palette of colors they embrace and the radiance they have because of the silk fibers. I fell in love with the rug in the window at the 4ᵗʰ Avenue Rug Gallery, walked inside and the rest is this history. The more I learn about rugs I realize there is so much more to know.

Zia Hassandeh (Herat Oriental Rugs) Alexandria, VA

Loves Heriz rugs, especially Serape's. They are primitive, not high kpsi, but have a beauty all their own. They are about 90 percent vegetable dyed and that gives them a unique color. How he got into the rug business is one of my favorite questions to ask. He said his father was exporting rugs from Afghanistan to Germany. In the 1980's he came to engineering school in Virginia. When he would go home to visit in Germany, he would bring back a few rugs to sell. He eventually found a warehouse and currently has about 25,000 rugs. No matter how many rugs you know, someone always brings you one that makes you wonder, "what is that"! It becomes difficult to understand if the rugs are vegetable or chemical.

Randy Hyde (Owner of Renaissance Rug Cleaning Past President & board member Association of Rug Care Specialists) OR

How you got in the rug business- I found the rug world by chance I was going to college part-time and needed a job, a family friend worked at a local cleaning & retail company (Atiyeh Brothers), and I got a job there. I didn't know anything about rugs or that there were handwoven rugs. I grew up in suburbia with wall-to-wall carpet. I remember thinking I would work for Atiyeh's for a year or two (it was 8 years) and then find a "real job" the work suited me, and rugs and the rug world made sense. What is the best lesson you learned? - Check your ego, and never hold a grudge in Business. What is your favorite rug and why? -May sound odd, but I really don't have one, I like lots of rugs for various reasons. I get to own customer rugs for a week or two and give them back. I have a customer that's a cat fanatic she would be a cat hoarder, she figured out how to channel that by working for at a rescue shelter so she can be the crazy cat lady without all the crazy cat issues, I kind of do the same with rugs.

Anthony Belmonte Studied at IICRC - Institute of Inspection, Cleaning and Restoration Certification

I don't know if could say I have a favorite rug, but I do tend to prefer the tribal and village rugs. I originally was in the carpet (wall to wall) cleaning business and started doing area rugs about 18 years ago and really moved into the oriental and area rug washing side of our business about 15 years ago, we currently only offer rug washing, no in home cleaning. My best takeaway would be that rug cleaning will never be boring, every rug is unique. No two rugs will clean the same. Stay on your toes and never stop learning.

Rob Decker (Managing Partner at Maxcare Carpet Cleaning and Repair)MO Studied Fiber theory and application to cleaning at WoolSafe North America

What is my favorite rug and why? My favorite rug would have to be antique Navajo weavings. The biggest reason for this, is that I love how the Navajo held great respect for their methods, ingredients, and the finished product. Never would harsh chemicals be a part of the process before the end user received their rug or blanket, as happens with so many other rugs from around the world. The result of this respectful attitude is a long lasting, skillfully crafted, piece of woven art. How did I end up in the Rug Business? I have been a carpet cleaner for 28 years. For the first 8-10 years, I was scared to clean rugs, for fear of bleeding or other issues. After that was about the time, I began to learn more about rugs, and the proper care, repair, and cleaning of them. Then, as so often happens, I got "bitten by the bug" and fell in love with the history, artistic mastery, and the look and feel of fine rugs. Without question, the time after I began my rug journey has been the most colorful part of a truly wonderful career. What is my best takeaway? I have been lucky enough to have met some of the finest people I have ever known through a common love of rugs. Some have been instructors, some fellow cleaners from around the globe, still other students, fostering lasting relationships that will be dear to me to my dying day. My takeaway would have to be "You meet the nicest people in a rug class".

Roberto Mora (President at Heirloom Oriental Rug Specialists) IL

Nain rugs are my favorite. I started as a regular laborer for a carpet cleaning company and when they sold off their business, I got started on having my own. My takeaway is all the beautiful art that is each individual hand-woven rug. I love admiring the artwork on them. Also, the number of friends that I have found in the business that want to help each other succeed.

Stephen Dusty (Team Leader at Luv-A-Rug Services Inc.) Victoria, Canada

My favorite rug is a Farahan sarouk. These have beautiful tones of warm reds in them, the handle is soft and exquisite plus I love how the field designs are not completely symmetrical showing that the weaver had a lot of latitude in the design. I also love how the dyes mellow with age and the tones become even nicer. Dad had a carpet cleaning company when I was a kid, and he would never touch a good rug. This piqued my interest when young and I started to self-educate on how to properly care for rugs as a young adult to the point of creating a whole line of very specialized commercial rug care equipment. My best lesson is how important it is to keep this artform alive. It is my duty to educate my clients to appreciate the skill, and passion that the weavers tie embeds into every Knot in their rugs. It is a big honor for me to tell them real stories about the people that wove their rugs and what a thrill I get when my clients thank me for the stories!

Nate Koets (Cleanorientalrug.com) MI

My favorite rug is a tribal, mixed technique piece, made in Konya, Turkey by Suzanne Yalcin, one of the two most skilled weavers I've ever had the pleasure to meet. It has 2-color (contrasting, black and white) goat hair warps and the weft colors change and alternate, complementing the design. As the rug wears the full beauty of her work will slowly be revealed. The pile is luxuriously long mohair and wool blend. It is unbelievably soft and the fully organic vegetal dyes just glow. Her husband is a dye-master and is passionate about the environment. He even threw shade at the DOBAG project, for not being organic and carbon-neutral, although he praised the good things they do.

I feel Suzanne's heart, soul, and spirit every time I see the rugs she created. There is an article written about her in HALI. I bought two of them, both scatter size, and one of those is a wall piece, with a braided tassel emerging from a flat woven panel in its center. The other is at my sisters in her entry. (It's on loan - I'd never sell it.) I gave the wall one to my best friend; we share the closest of bonds and have since we were children.

I got into the rug cleaning business by accident. accident. I was a 2nd gen installed carpet cleaner asked to clean a silk/silk Persian Qum in 1991. I knew better than to try. I sent my client to Chicago, but my dad started looking in earnest for an oriental rug cleaning school. In 1992 he saw a 1" classified ad from Phil Auserehl and Ron Toney, advertising their first rug washing class, held in Berthoud, CO that same year.

The school was built around first learning the science of rug cleaning, so that one can select and achieve the best result possible, regardless of method. Their system is proprietary, built around the Auserehlian purpose-made dusting and washing air tools, with each tool designed to harness the laws of physics unique to that environment air or water.

The education is to this day, unmatched and unrivaled. Phil and Ron Toney taught us to think outside the box as a mindset, day-to-day. The only constant in the rug cleaning world, is change. My best lesson from rugs is: You can't outperform your education. Have a plan, and a backup plan, custom made with the needs and weaknesses unique to each textile in mind. Above all, a rug washer must do no harm.

Jason Nazimyal (Gallery Owner, Nazmiyal) NYC, New York

Favorite rugs are those with primitive tribal designs. Rugs like Gabbehs that before the 1980's wasn't' known to the rest of the world. His most favorite is a very rare piece he calls an ambiguous rug. There is a uniqueness of pattern and a clarity of the weave.

Look here to see his favorite rug!

His story of how I got into the rug industry is a combination of desperation and family connections. While in College he started working with his cousin who was established in the business in the NYC area. He went with his cousin on a delivery during spring break to an area called Short Hills, NJ. He sold two rugs. His cousin asked him if he would be interested in opening a shop with him on Milbourn Ave in this area. He said yes and that was the beginning. He was in various partnerships with his cousin and with his brothers. Over the years it evolved into each of them focusing on different parts of the business. His specialty and love are for antique rugs.

His lesson he has learned is that rugs are a school where the lesson never ends. You reach a point where the rugs speak to you. He is a hunter of rugs. He can look at a catalog of thousands of pieces, but there is the one that speaks to him, loud and clear.

Richard Inman (Owner Rich's Fine Oriental Rugs) AZ

His most favorite rug is those from Bijar. He values them for their richness of color, durability, and their longevity. He loves the quality of the rugs. He started collecting rugs around 2000. They began to fill his house and he decided to open a shop. With a passion for rugs and no business sense, he had a shop from 2005-2011. The best part was about educating his clients about rugs. His lesson was its not the best idea of opening a rug store and to be careful. Understanding the true value of rugs is just as complicated as their construction.

Mitch McLemore (Jonquil Rug Cleaning Co.) GA

Favorite rug: Although there are so many that I love, I would probably lean more to the Heriz. I love the rich color hues, chunky knots, and range of geometric and floral/leaf patterns. How did we end up in the rug business? My wife and I lived in Turkey for many years, so we were surrounded by and fell in love with all the many beautiful rugs there! What have I learned? Every rug has a story to tell- from the region it came from and the weaver's design, to the journey of various owners of the rug. The beautiful thing about hand woven rugs is that they are just like people. - no two are alike!

CHAPTER 3

WHAT'S MY RUG?

What's My Rug is a Facebook Group that is committed to help in rug identification. Each rug is as individual as a fingerprint! Each of us in the different facets of rug world have our own story for entering what is our common thread? Our passion. Let's start at the beginning of understanding rugs. Their individual properties are intertwined in the fibers of which they are made.

What's my Rug?

What is my rug? Do you know?

Help me to discover the wonder in my hands!

Help me to see how hands of magic wove these threads!

Tell me what you see. Teach me what you know!

Finely woven, expertly dyed, you are holding a piece of our collective history.

When you ask and I answer, a whole wonderful story will emerge.

CHAPTER 4

FIBERS

We begin with fibers. Most of my experiences are with natural fibers: wool, silk, cotton. There are also other fibers such as jute or camel or goat hair. Weavers are some of the most creative people I have ever met. They think in colors, fibers, symbols. They have in a language full of dreams. This idea has been over ten years in the making. I attribute it to the fact that the more I know the more there is necessary to learn. Thread by thread I went from writing one poem to describe the rug in front of me to dedicating hours of research to fill in the facts. This poem has been my overall thought that I have shared with rug lovers, friends, clients and tourists and poets to share my passion. This next poem is my title and one of the first poems I wrote about rugs.

Weaving Life
Fabulous and phenomenal fibers.
Art is all around.
Love is in their looms.
Why rugs can enchant one heart and have no effect on another?
The gift is vision.
If you can see the hidden world, the rugs can tell the story,
A thousand stories. A life in every knot.
Love in every warp and weft.
A love that endures time.
The history of the past, the present and the future woven by hand.
Is that why the fates are described as spinning the yarn of our destinies?
Every knot is measured even before we are born.

When we clean carpets, we understand that learning how they were made, and the origins of the fibers and the dyes plays the most important role. How fibers are processed deeply affects how they can be cleaned. Quite fascinating to read about the wool industry in the top weaving countries, as you will see.

From the tribal folks of the Bakhtiari tribe to the industrialized looms of India, the whole process begins with living animals the sheep, goats, camels, alpaca and the like whose fur makes up a large part of the industry. I took a class in textiles back in 2005. At the Interior Design Program at Mesa College. Here's some information from my report!

Wool

Wool begins its life story during the Stone Age about 10,000 years ago with Mesopotamian Plain inhabitants had sheep for three things: food, clothing, and shelter. Between 3000 and 1000 BC the Persians, Greeks and Romans had wool trade in Europe. Romans took sheep everywhere as they built their Empire in Spain, North Africa, and on the British Isles. The first wool processing plant was in England as early as 50 AD. After that the Saracens had wool trade with North Africa, Greece, Egypt, and Constantinople which led to weaving in Florence, Genoa, and Venice. Venice then began conquest of Greece and prospered with slaves to do its weaving. Controlling the wool industry in the 12th and 13th century was very important as its industry meant power.

Sheep were brought to Cuba and Santo Domingo in 1493, and Cortez brought them when he traveled to what is now Mexico. Navajo and other Indian tribes are famous for their woolen rugs. In North America a few sheep had grown into a heard of about 100,000 by 1665. In those days Massachusetts even passed a law requiring young people to spin and weave. Traditions were created. The spinning duties fell to the eldest unmarried daughter in the family, giving birth to the word "spinster."

Yarn was wound on a reel (weasel) which made a popping sound when released and began that famous verse: Pop goes the weasel! Early presidents Washington and Jefferson kept flocks of sheep; both were wearing woolen suits on the day of their inauguration.

New inventions like the spinning machines grew the industry rapidly as we approach the 18th century and small flocks started the industry in Australia, New Zealand, and South Africa. Iran was the largest manufacturer of wool in the 18th century.

Since that time other countries began to purchase wool from Iran. In the 19th century places such as Istanbul, Baghdad, India, Russia began purchasing wool from Iran.

By the 1940's almost 25,000 people were employed in the textile industry. In Iran wool has also been used for bedding, tents, wrapping materials besides carpets. The production today in Iran is about 50,000 tons of wool per year and they rank 5th worldwide for production. These days much of the handmade popular rugs are from Afghanistan. One of the first documented industries there is Adeem Wardak Wool Washing and Carpet weaving factory in 1932.

The daily production is about 4,000 kilograms. There is room for expansion and that is a matter of power and land. Previously combined with Pakistani products, the new production with thanks to equipment from China is a higher quality product. The availability of such a facility has greatly improved the industry in that area.

Speaking of China, they have been leading in the efficiency of wool processing and have bought most of Australia's output. This due to cost: processing in China is much cheaper than in Europe, and since Merino wool is the best wool in the world, their competitive prices keep the high-quality products available there. Wool in India on the other hand is a very rural industry.

Wool is the only natural fiber in which they are deficient, and you will see a prevalence of jute and cotton in their rugs as a result. 85% of their wool production in India is carpet grade. The world average for wool productivity is about 3.5 kilograms per year per sheep compare that to the average in India which is 0.8 kilograms per year. That is the reason for the creation of Indian Wool Improvement Program. Sheep are practical as an investment. All parts are used as wool is a renewable commodity and they provide meat. Sheep thrive everywhere: all 50 states and most countries. The terrain they can exist in is incredible! Most live-in areas devoid of normal crops and in high elevations. Sheep can survive and thrive on weeds and roots that other animals don't eat, therefore they are environmentally economical as well.

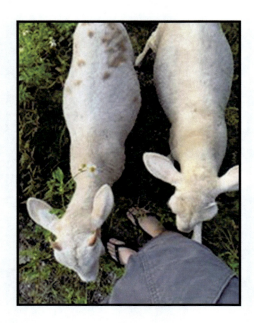

Wool Products Labeling Act, states that textiles made with wool must list the source of their fibers. Wool is essentially protein made of amino acids, they are far more complex than cellulose and as such have many more ways to react with chemical dyes. Acid Dyes require some things to be careful about: they are sensitive to high pH so you cannot use the high soda ash recipes that one uses to dye cotton. Usually, an acid is used in the dyeing process.

Wool is typically dyed including heat in the recipes as it incurs the best results with caution as this process takes place as the acid recipe is reactive. Stainless steel is the vessel of choice. Vat Dyes are used when doing some the natural dyes such indigo as the fibers must sit and absorb the dye but can't be at a pH too high. Natural Dyes work extremely well on wool fibers but with a mordant of metal like copper, alum, tin, or iron. Facts about working with wool can be summarized by its properties. Most wool is subject to shrinkage unless you are dealing with a chemically washed wool. Be careful of inducing sudden temperature changes as this may affect the wool's resiliency. Mohair is from angora goats that takes dyes beautifully as does Cashmere.

They pick up intense colors easily and are less likely to exhibit felting or matting together as their structure is quite fine. When talking about sheep's wool, luster wools such as Cotswold, Lincoln and Romney are used for making carpets as they are hardwearing. Shorter wools are more typically used for clothing like merino, Rambouillet and Polwarth.

Wool has good resiliency when it is dry, but not when wet so one must be cautious about any mechanical tension applied while wet. Sometimes when we talk about wool, we mention the term angora. There are two different types of Angora wool. That which is from goats and that from rabbits. Goat angora goes into the making of rugs. Rabbit angora goes into the clothing industry. And of course, for something completely different we have angora cats! To introduce to Angora rugs let's begin with a bit of history. The first we heard of the breed is between the 12th and 15th centuries B.C. The name "Angora" came from Ankara, Turkey, where the Angora goat became well established. Angora rabbits and Angora cats also were developed in the same province in Turkey. Angora goats produce "mohair" which is derived from the Arabic word "mukhaya" which means to choose or prefer. The hair of the Angora goat is not to be confused with "Angora" fiber which comes from Angora rabbits. We hear that white silky mohair was a coveted fiber even in biblical references where Moses mentions the breed in roughly 1500 BC. Early Angora goat owners carefully protected their Angora goats who often lived inside the family homes just as any other precious pet.

Angora goats were brought to Europe about 1554 but exports from Turkey in those early references were unsuccessful. The Sultan of Turkey placed a strict embargo on further exports of Angora goats or mohair in the 15th century. Some finished products made of mohair were still exported and interest in obtaining Angora goats grew.

Some exportations to Spain and France took place in the late 18th century again with limited success. In 1883 the existing embargo was eventually lifted, and Angora goats were exported to South Africa. Angora goats were crossed with hardy local breeds and the Angora goat breeding industry thrived. Angora goats were not introduced to the United States until 1849 with the importation of 7 does and 2 bucks. By the 1960's, the US had over 5 million commercial white Angora goats with more than 90% of mohair produced in Texas.

The number of Angora goats in Texas has steadily decreased (to 1.8 million in 1992 and to less than 200,000 as of May 2009) at least in part due to the elimination of the mohair subsidy and expanded use of synthetic fibers. South Africa has now passed the US in mohair production. Growing interest in natural products has returned interest to this fiber. While large commercial herds of Angora goats are diminishing, their desirability for small family farms continues to grow. Colored Angora goats and mohair in a variety of natural colors further increase the appeal of Angora goats.

History of Angora rabbit breeds starts during the time of the Romans. According to www.angoras.co.uk. It is thought that the Romans kept, bred, and utilized Angora wool since at least 100 BC and were established in Eastern Europe around 500 - 600 AD as best as can be determined, possibly brought there by the Romans.

The tribes living in the chilly Carpathian Mountains of Transylvania (between Romania and Hungary) maintained herds of captive Angoras and bred them for their warm wool. The tribes also had goats for their mohair fibers, but the angora rabbit wool was infinitely softer, warm, and lightweight than the mohair. (BTW, the Romans had a large presence in the region for hundreds of years. Even today you'll find extensive evidence of Roman occupation throughout Europe, and an entire people-group called the Romansch living in Switzerland's mountainous Canton Graubunden. Their language, also called Romansch, is still spoken, and is one of 4 equally recognized languages in Switzerland.)

Sometimes my own story surprises me as I had a dear friend from Sion, Switzerland who spoke Romansch! I spoke English, Greek, some Polish and some French and she spoke French, German, Romansch, Greek and some English and some Italian. We both were married to Greeks and would usually compare the words in every language! One of my best life road trips was with Francoise and my sister Elisabeth.

Elisabeth and I left Greece by plane to Rome. We trained to Florence, then Bologna, (because Venice had rain and had floods) then Venice then through the Alps to Sion. After a tour of the region including Zermatt and Geneva my sister flew to Los Angeles. Francoise and I began another journey! We drove from the Alps (we had snow in October!) down into Italy stopping in Modena for gourmet items. We drove to Ancona, Italy where we took the ferry to Corfu. Or spouses were there we went swimming as it was still quite favorable weather. We stopped in Ithaca to see the palace of Odysseus (of the Odyssey fame) and made our way back to Athens. Travel is an amazing teacher!

Angora rabbits were called *Angolas* for over a millennium, until as recently as the 1800's in some locales. *'Angola'* was the word the Romanian tribes used to describe the rabbit wool. It meant "un-scratchy. To get from sheep to wool fibers, there are many processes involved.

The one I would like to highlight here is spinning. Most people do not even think about the spinning process when they see a carpet. Spinning is more important than weaving in the production of a high-quality carpet. Wool spinning is a highly technologically developed process even when using primitive equipment. This process applies only to wool, camel, goat, or other animal fibers.

Even though the process of spinning plant fibers, such as cotton or linen, may look the same from the outside, they are technically quite different. Processing and spinning silk are entirely different processes which we will talk about later.

In most of the early tribes, there were two types of spinners: those for warps and those for wefts because of the different types of processes required of the materials and this crafted different pinning techniques. Combed wool is used in producing warp. Wool cards produce warp threads, only when most all the fibers are aligned. This wool can be spun into a yarn that is strong and smooth. Warp is not soft because the spinner must put a little bit of extra twist into it to get the strength. Finished warp threads will be placed vertically on the loom and held under tension, so that typically more than one single strand is plied. Twisting two strands together for strength in the way one makes a wire cable, guaranteeing that the warp will not break as the rug is being woven. When we look closely at this spinning technique, it is done so that the fibers remain in a line as they are being spun. Only weavers with a high amount of skill produce warp threads. The spinning of weft threads is a more general process, fibers can softer and it's not crucial that the fibers remain in perfect alignment. Young wool spinners are given this process as weft requires less skill. After wool is spun, the next step is the dyeing process.

One of the most widely used fibers is polyester. Polyester is a very durable manufactured fiber used in both wall to wall carpeting as well as area rugs. It is solution dyed and therefore very resistant to bleaching, fading and other wear and tear. It is inexpensive and can be created in various forms like loop or cut pile and is widely used in commercial applications. It is however is difficult to dye, so colors and patterns are more limited.

Polyester also is not oil-resistant, so these types of stains become permanent. Cotton is another fiber that dyes easily and allows for many colors. It is used primarily in area rugs and patterns are created in a braided or flat weave, and they are a softer alternative to jute or sisal rugs. Durable, most often they are machine washable.

Cotton fibers makes the rugs less expensive than wool rugs and are not as formal as wool rugs tend to be, this makes them a good choice for busy families on a budget. Olefin rugs have been in the industry for a long time. It is considered the most popular manufactured fiber used in rugs. It is stain-resistant, holds color well but it can over time get matted. With its durability and ability to repel stains and moisture, olefin is often used in outdoor settings.

Jute and sisal are one of the most appealing natural fibers used in rugs. These fibers create tough, very durable rugs. The construction of these rugs allows for textures and weaves that other types of fiber normally cannot achieve. Jute and sisal are a good alternative if someone has a wool allergy. They are however since they are rough on your feet compared to wool or cotton rugs. It is difficult to remove stains since they absorb any type of moisture. Difficult to seam, they are best suited for area rugs.

Silk and viscose are very soft, easy to dye and absorbent materials. Though they are versatile, they are not very durable on their own. They work well in a combination with wool. Their fibers create depth and give rugs a beautiful sheen.

As you know 100% silk rugs are costly and need extreme care in cleaning and dyeing. They are typically used as an accent rug or wall hanging because of this, though silk as a fiber is very strong. One of the most amazing stories in my life was because of a silk rug. While working at the rug gallery, a family came in asking if we could help with sewing a backing on 100% silk rug quickly. Their daughter was taking command of a ship in the Navy, and she wanted to have it as a decoration. We were able to make that happen, and as a result, I was invited to a change of command ceremony in the Naval shipyard. What an amazing honor, like so many incredible experiences in my life are a result of knowing about rugs.

How to differentiate the types of silk rugs?

Great question! There are a few types of handmade rugs in the realm of silk. The one we know the most about is the Persian Qum, nearly 100% are 100% silk. There are other Persian rugs that incorporate silk in their foundations like Isfahan and Tabriz. There are others that may use silk accents like Bijar or Nain.

You can easily see the fibers when looking at the back of the rug. Handmade rugs are easy to identify as the back is a mirror of the front. You can do a knot count as silk rugs are much finer.

Fringe is the warp and weft unfinished, and usually decoratively finished. If it isn't handmade your fringe will be glued on, sewed on, a piece of fabric, then it isn't the original fringe and the rug possibly may be machine made.

NATURAL SILK is made from fibers harvested from silk caterpillars: 2,500 caterpillars= 1 pounds of silk.

ART SILK or artificial silk is a synthetic fiber which resembles silk, but costs less to produce. We usually equate artificial silk with Rayon.

BAMBOO SILK is a viscose made from bamboo.

BAGHALAPOUR SILK is silk made in a small town on the banks of the river Ganja. Which now has the name silk city.

KASHMIR SILK rugs are renowned to have bright, jewel-like color tones such as sapphire blue, ruby red, emerald green, aquamarine, amethyst, and ivory. Rugs from Kashmir are traditionally made in oriental, floral designs that typically involve the significant and culturally important motifs such as the paisley, chinar tree, (the oriental plane) and tree-of-life. Most of these designs are rooted in the Kashmiri way of life and are a symbolic representation of the age-old Kashmir tradition of hospitality, warmth, and love.

It is often said in Kashmir folklore that a home is incomplete without a soul - a Kashmir carpet. The ethos of Kashmir culture is often represented in the motifs of a Kashmir rug. Although, the art of making these gorgeous rugs is not native to Kashmir and was first introduced nearly 400 years back by the Mughal rulers in India. Yet the indigenous brilliance of the local crafts-persons has made Kashmir carpets one of the most sought after works of art in the world. They can be 100% silk or a combination.

Viscose is the textile industry's answer to silk. Originally used as a n accent fiber, nowadays it is one of the most popular choices for designer rugs." Many in the rug cleaning industry are against viscose rugs and refuse to service those rugs as they don't want to support that industry. I take the unpopular stance of specializing in restoring Viscose rugs, since I believe that in doing so, I'm decreasing the demand for these types of rugs. This is my way to keep additional viscose rugs from entering the market." Issa Hoker

Nylon which can transform into a limitless number of colors. It resists dirt and grime and can easily clean it. It is a very strong that stands up to heavy traffic. It has a silky appearance. Nylon is often acid dyed which results in fading and other long-term issues, and in high-traffic areas tend to show soiling and pressure and furniture marks. The newest fiber is Triexta. Invented by DuPont, Triexta is currently produced exclusively by Du Pont. Mohawk Industries is currently the biggest manufacturer to use Sorona (triexta) in carpet, and it markets the fiber under its brand name Smart Strand. Hirst, a much smaller manufacturer based out of Australia, also uses Sorona in its eco+ line of carpets.

The technical name for Triexta is polytrimethylene terephthalate or PTT for short. Triexta is naturally very stain resistant. Can be cleaned with only water, rather than using a spot cleaner, it holds its appearance extremely well. Softer than both polyester and nylon because it does not have chemicals applied to the fiber for stain protection. DuPont began using biotechnology based on fermentation of corn glucose replacing up to 37 percent in DuPont Sorona. Corn glucose is much more sustainable than petroleum. Fewer chemicals are put into the fiber, which in turn means that fewer chemicals will come out of the fiber in the form of VOCs (off-gassing).Even the Berber type of designs that feel rough feel soft to the touch when made with Triexta.

The Weaver's Tale

Sipping tea as the dampness at dusk settles. The beginning of winter is around the corner. Sitting with the rugs, sitting with myself.

Like a traveler between worlds, my pen writes the words that are just on the horizon. Time passes and stops to say hello.

Did you remember to reflect? It stops to ask.

The textiles piled here and there, there and here.

The movement of the world measured by threads.

Sitting with myself, craving the gentle embrace of a warm-hearted lover to break the chill of my mood.

Before I would call, now I am called, to understand and interpret the designs from another time and place. Infinity rests with me.

Chapter 5

NATURAL DYES

This subject is so vast and varies from country to country, weaving group to weaving group. Here's some of my favorite facts about the process.

Being an avid color enthusiast, it was exceptional to find information explaining in depth about vegetable dye sources in the East. So much of village dyeing information is passed from generation to generation without many westerners ever understanding their origins. When looking at what is written about fabric dyeing, there are many angles to approach from. With modern technology we are beginning to understand their chemical composition, document which plants and what they come from, and a bit about the overall longevity of the colors. Most of the popular dyes have much written about their stories: indigo, red madder, cochineal. Even much has been discussed about using iron shavings or walnut shells to create black dyes. Today's topic is shades of gold and yellow from plant materials. At first, I thought that saffron, the costly floral media was used in the process, now I discovered a whole array of plants that dyes are made of in the rug making regions. I will give you a glimpse of a hidden world.

Most of this information is gathered from chemists that are rug crazy. The works of Harald Bohmer and Dr. Helmut Schweppe are expansive to say the least especially in conjunction with vegetable dye enthusiasts in Turkey and Germany. As we all well know, so much of the history of rugs and related topics is in the style of the troubadour handed down by word-of-mouth generation to generation. Color is a sensation that occurs when light hits the retina, and the brain responds. It has been discovered that there are people who see yellow because of an extra cone cell for it, in addition to seeing green, violet to blue and red to orange. This results in finer distinction of the other three colors. We will discuss all the natural plants that can create dyes and a few known facts about them.

I am firm believer in divine coincidence.

Many of my somewhat seeming odd experiences fit into my weaving story perfectly. One of the positions I had in Greece was in a spice factory. To me, the wafting aromas of grinding spices is something I can conjure now. I can have one of those synesthetic memories of the smell of cumin, cinnamon, and nutmeg grinding! Because it ties many of my cultural experiences together, I will start with saffron.

Saffron

The most expensive from the crocus of the flower has been cultivated 3000 yrs. Found in Morocco, Spain, Iran, Greece, Kashmir, Switzerland. Beautiful shade of light yellow.

Safflower

This flower creates both red and yellow dyes. This dye was predominantly in the historical "Polish carpets" from the 16th and 17th centuries. I find this fascinating as I am 100% Polish and see that through history, Poland as a nation has greatly appreciated the arts. These rugs were made in Persia and given to Polish Royalty and have survived to the present time. The plants are found in West Asia, North Africa, and Europe.

There are so many variations to achieve yellow. I thought of skipping through this, but the truth is depending where you live some flowers are more predominant than others!

Dyer's weed: Weld

The leaves from the second year can produce dye. It has been known since Roman times and is extremely colorfast. It is native to West Asia and the Mediterranean, can dye both wool and silk in a very deep yellow.

Three leaf sage

Used for tea in the Mediterranean, grows very well in Turkey and in Greece. The leaves and shoots create a much muted yellow.

Monk's Pepper Tree: Chaste Tree

Spicy smelling bush has fruit that is like pepper that is known to curb the libido. Grown in Europe, W. Asia, and the Mediterranean produces a greenish yellow.

Dyer's Greenwort

Known since the Middle Ages as a dye source, it is best known as the plant used with indigo to produce green. Found in Turkey and throughout Europe makes a deep shade of yellow.

Spartium Juncean

With no English translation is a medicinal plant primarily found in the Canary Islands and Southern Europe and Mediterranean makes a medium yellow.

Until getting into the nature of dyes, I knew Chamomile as a tea and Herbal remedy!

Chamomile

The daisy family has many types that produce dye

1. Anthemis Chia Anatolia, S. Europe

2. Anthemis tomentosa Italy, Sicily, Anatolia

3. Golden Marguerite "Dyers Chamomile" Europe, Himalayas, Turkey, S. Asia

4. Tripleuspermum maritimum (scentless chamomile) Europe, S. Turkey

5. True Chamomile strong scent makes deep shades of yellow, found in E. Europe, Turkey, Caucasus, Siberia, Iran; Afghanistan can also be a tea.

6. Anacyclus claratus Turkey, S. Europe, N. Africa

Chrysanthemum

Chrysanthemum Coronarium has a deep yellow orange dye which is not affected much by light from Mediterranean to Iran under the olive trees. Growing up we grew Chrysanthemums in the back-yard garden. If only knew then of their healing and dyeing properties!

Yarrow

Found in very rocky soil in the Mediterranean and Europe strong yellow dye. Living in Rhodes, I would take 5-mile walks around the island in the morning. At the time I worked in Anatoli Spice Company and began to recognize many of the common Mediterranean herbs as I walked. Yarrow was very prevalent!

Thyme

There are over 38 species in Turkey alone and as such is widely used by village dyers. Very common all over the Mediterranean. The plants create a solid yellow. As it is also popular as a seasoning, so many have it in their personal gardens.

Foxglove (Digitalis)

Poisonous causes toxic reactions and used as a pharmaceutical because of its cardiac glycosides. Does make a great shade of yellow but not widely used because of the danger.

Phlomis (Mint Family) Found everywhere in Turkey and the Steppes creates a pleasing shade of yellow. Mint as you know is one the easiest to grow herbs. One plant will easy expand in all the empty spaces!

Daphne Oleosides

Can be toxic though it is used in the treatment of gout and rheumatism. Found in Asia, S. Europe. Really strong shade of yellow widely used in the 1960's in Turkey.

Barberry

Most remembered for the dye used to color the tents of the Turkish army and is known as early as the 14th century. Is medium lightfast and to dye use the roots and bark. It is also used in Cooking

Anatolian Buckthorn

Turkish Dyestuff used since the 15th century the color is made from the berries.

Sorrel

Otherwise known as Rumex from the Himalayas. Dyes created range from yellow to brown. Not so common so rarely used. Sometimes eaten as a salad or soup!

Hemp

Used as a dye plant in Turkey, the Caucasus, and Northern India. The whole plant is used to make a yellowish orange that is conditionally lightfast.

Dyer's Sumac

Creates a yellow orange dye was used in the older days to dye leather. My former mother-in-law worked in the leather industry. We had these amazing samples of South American leather, and some were yellow. I love how writing this book is piecing the puzzle of my own story.

Sicilian Sumac

Also known as tanner's sumac. The berries are used as a spice in the Middle east especially Persia. High tannin content deep yellow not lightfast on wool.

Pomegranate

Known as the apple from Adam and Eve. Widely used by the Romans and Phoenicians and the fruit that Paris gave Aphrodite. It's the apple in Buddhist and Islamic art. It can make yellow, yellow brown, and black

Helichrysum

Strawflowers 18 species in Turkey alone. Produces a shade of yellow/orange.

Inula Viscosa

Found mostly near Bergama Good lightfastness and creates a very intense yellow

Rock roses

Used as a dye in the Ankara area makes a yellow to green shade

Wine Grape

fresh leaves are used for cooking and produce a yellow that is not light fast.

Turpentretra

Also known as the wild pistachio in the Mediterranean makes a light yellow.

Common Onion

The skins of the fruit have been known since antiquity, but the dye isn't lightfast used to dye eggs in some countries. My maternal grandmother would boil onion skins to dye eggs a lovely shade of purple that became brown with further boiling.

Euphorbia rigida

One of the 90 species of spurge has horizontal leaves that are toxic but produce a intense yellow.

Hypercium empertrifolium also known as St John's wort makes a pale shade of yellow.

Mullein (candlewick)

Very toxic plant that makes yellow hair dye. Found in Scandinavia, Turkey, Asia, N. Africa. Great color but not used because of the toxicity.

Dyes are very key in the world of handmade rugs. Many people are intimately involved with indigo, there are medicinal uses for the plant. Indigo in some cultures is used for the healing of wounds. Books have been written about it and is said to impart protection to the skin. The famous Tuareg "blue people" of the Sahara whose wearing vast amounts of this hues give their skin a blue cast that is proven. Dyestuffs that are roots and are sold for their medicinal properties like red madder. It is known to heal the stomach and kidneys. Sumac is a dye and a rice flavoring accent in Turkish and Persian restaurants. Turmeric a popular yellow dye is known for its healing properties and is widely used as an anti-inflammatory! Sandalwood is dye for fabric and more commonly known as a colorant for cosmetics.

Tribal groups that use natural dyes do this as they are readily available as opposed to the properties of artificial dyes. Artificial dyes since the 1800's have been widely available but because of their toxic contraindications are the exception in the dye process in the more tribal rural cultures of fabric.

There are historical references to Tyrian Purple, in the days of the Roman Empire and the trading of the Phoenicians. When I lived on the island of Rhodes there was a historical dig where they would do the dyeing for this amazing hue. It was made from the boiling of murex snail shells. The British Empire was pushing into

Africa in the 1850's. The Empire's colonization journeys were beaten back by malaria. Quinine that comes from cinchona trees come mostly from South America was found to cure malaria and scientists wanted a better way to get their hands on the drug. William Perkins, a young chemist joined the Royal Academy of Sciences was a prodigy at 15. In 1856 "Perkin produced little more than a black, sticky mess "while trying to synthesize quinine. When he went to dissolve his gunk in alcohol, it revealed a deep purple liquid. Perkin's purple, otherwise known as aniline purple, was the first synthetic dye. The synthesis transformed purple's elite status, and probably saved the lives of a great many snails.

Many of the red known dyes come from plant sources (red madder) and from the insect world as well! Both Cochineal and Lac come from specific insects! We find ourselves in the Rug Room talking about dyes and how they affect the cleaning process. In my quest for some additional thought for my book, "Weaving Life" in the editing stage, I saw an article from back 1988 about Armenian Red dye, and I became curious. As you know, some of the first rugs to come into the American market were Sarouks that became painted red to make them more acceptable to the population.

There are a few red dyes we are in acquaintance with, especially Red madder. Madder Red was one of the most important textile colorants used in the Industrial Revolution. It was also, in the form of Turkey or Adrianople Red, a triumph of Islamic technology. Red madder is also in the news for being as a crop with renewable qualities and planted with this intention.

Three centuries ago, Europeans considered Turkey Red to be one of the great wonders of the Orient. This brilliant and fiery color applied to cotton was much admired for its durability and fastness. The birthplace of Turkey Red was the Near East, from whence it had traveled to India. The dyestuff was from the root of the madder plant. Working with this color involved 'numerous and tedious operations' and were also harsh, which meant that only the best quality cotton could be used. Despite tremendous efforts, Turkey Red dyeing could not be mastered to any extent in Western Europe, even after Greek dyers were brought to France, and some European dyers sent spies to the Levant. Around 1745 Greek dyers based in Marseille introduced a version of the color, and their process was taken up in Rouen. In 1756 Levantine dyers were brought to Saint Chamoun in the Loire region, and it was not long before details of their processes were carried to Lyon.

The most widely known red is from cochineal. Originally from Spanish America, it's an insect that feeds on cactus. Widely used in the textiles of Turkey, the Caucasus, and India. Mesoamerican peoples in southern Mexico had started using the cochineal bug as early as 2000 BCE, long before the arrival of the conquistadors, according to Mexican textile expert Quetzalina Sanchez. Indigenous people in Puebla, Tlaxcala, and Oaxaca had systems for breeding and engineering the cochineal bugs for ideal traits and the pigment was used to create paints for codices and murals, to dye cloth and feathers, and even as medicine.

The color Lac is from India and other parts of Asia, which is used in Indian textiles and shellac. It is a natural dye that is extracted from scale insects (*Kerria lacca*) found in Asia. Lac, used as a natural dye for hundreds of years and is very sensitive to pH, an increase in alkalinity turns the colors plum purple, while acidity gives bright oranges. However, colors that have been modified by a change in pH can change back to red after rinsing. Working with it you will get reds from lac, ranging from crimson to burgundy. Lac reds are softer and warmer than cochineal reds. A pinch of iron modifies the colors towards purple.

Kermes red is derived from the dried bodies the *Kermes* insects that are native in the Mediterranean region and live on the sap of a Kermes Oak. They were used as a red dye by the ancient Greeks and Romans. The kermes dye is a rich red, a crimson. It has staying power in silk and wool. It was much esteemed in the medieval era for dyeing silk and wool. Post-medieval it was replaced by other red dyes, like cochineal. It is also known as Polish red.

The color "Armenian red" is from Ararat Cochineal. The Armenian cochineal, also known as the Ararat cochineal or Ararat scale, is a scale insect indigenous to the Ararat plain and Aras River valley in the Armenian Highlands. It was formerly used to produce an eponymous crimson carmine dyestuff known in Armenia as Vordan karmir and historically in Persia as kirmiz. It is possible that Armenian cochineal dye was in use as early as 714 BC.

CHAPTER 6

COLORS

I differentiated dyes from colors, as perceiving color is more of a personal and physical process for the one that is seeing them. Colors have been thought to be of a mystical nature and represent different stories when chosen as a thread color for weaving. Here is one of my favorite quotes about color: "Mere color unspoiled by meaning and unadulterated with definite forms, can speak to the soul in a thousand different ways.'" Oscar Wilde. That's a part about rugs that is the most difficult to put in words, the way a specific color or pattern speaks to the soul and you just want to have it. Here's a little information to help explain that concept.

Compare to a world where everything is gray, nothing excites all our senses like color. It elicits a feeling. When we see color, it transmits to your body energetic input as well as neural and physiological. Color is not a science or a perception exactly, its almost a language we as soul speak. It is like intuition and its imagery came before humanity developed words. Color is a subjective experience, as each of us perceives it in a totally different way. The source of all color is light. Way back in college I took a class called Light and Vision. Interesting to me now how so many of my unique experiences, like this class, have been intrinsic to my knowledge and appreciation of textiles, though I may not have realized it at the time.

Robert Boyle was the first scientist to relate color to light. This is best explained that we describe light according to the color spectrum. The colors being: red, orange, yellow, green, blue, indigo, violet, with white being all color and black an absence of color.

Color theory is used to repair the tones of rugs. Here is a rug color correction from Rug Colorist, Issa Hoker. "Red dye bleed. Here I used color theory to get rid of the red color. Rug dyeing isn't just to dye faded colors, but also can be used to correct a color, such as in this case, instead of using harsh dye strippers."

The world relates to color with a few filters whether its cultural, religious, spiritual, biological, or psychological. The silent language of color has had many ways to define it. Books have noted 50,000 different hues and values of color! Color speaks about our shared values of beauty, nature, power, authority, faith, caste, marriage, rank, valor, and nationalism.

I speak in Color, I think in Symbols

I speak in color; I think in symbols. My vision guides my life!

Colors are my universe.

Dreaming nomad dreams.

The universal language is woven.

The weaver is an artist.

Beautiful wishes and nature's wonders.

I see so clearly.

I speak in color; I think in symbols.

I hear your thoughts. I share your vision.

Expressing life's wonders.

Soul has a dream that words cannot easily describe.

Thinking in the symbols that all of humanity knows.

Seeing color as emotion and feeling.

Sensing the light and sound that together create a vision.

I speak in color; I think in symbols!

The power of colors to emit a feeling or express a mood has even been studied by cognitive scientists. The human eye can perceive millions of different colors, but the number of categories human languages use to group those colors is much smaller. Some languages use as few as three color categories (words corresponding to black, white, and red), for instance if you have seen the art of tribal groups in North Africa, and I have also had art from the Rainforest Indians and from some Aborigine groups. All of it is in shades of red, white, and black. While the languages of industrialized cultures use up to 10 or 12 categories. Languages tend to divide the "warm" part of the color spectrum into more color words, such as orange, yellow, and red, compared to the "cooler" regions, which include blue and green. Across more than 100 languages, this finding may reflect the fact that most objects that stand out in a scene are warm-colored, while cooler colors such as green and blue tend to be found in backgrounds, the researchers say. Every language has this amazing similar ordering of colors, so that reds are more consistently communicated than greens or blues.

Different colors had different meanings and different weavers picked with intention colors to convey through their pattern and designs and were more than just a decorative element. Different colors had different meanings and different weavers choose their colors deliberately depending on the message they wanted to convey through their pattern and design. Persian weavers believe green is a holy color as it is associated with the Prophet Mohammed and as a result use it green sparingly. It was usually reserved for those sections of the rug that were unlikely to be walked on very often, such as the corners and sides. Green in other places is the color of hope, life, spring, and renewal. Blue symbolizes a sense of strength and or force. It stands for power, honesty and solitude and alludes to the afterlife. Weavings in yellow is associated with the sun and represents the joy of life and living. Orange is used to add a touch of humility or piety to the design. I read somewhere about the weaving beliefs from Bali. Many of the islands weave as well.

I was excited to have attended an online presentation:

Woven Dreams from Sacred Mountains: Textile Traditions of the Tboli & Blaan of Mindanao" by the Textile Museum Associates of Southern California, Inc. and saw the amazing way Ikat textile is created. Most weavers feel a divine purpose in their task, pick patterns and materials to create their art. Most traditional weavers attribute a certain power or feeling to the colors they choose. I did some research and found some amazing Insights!

Some of the attributes weavers and healers give a certain specific color:

Pink- Love, caring, life force

Aqua- Mental and emotional calm

Sky Blue- Knowing, sensing spirituality

Navy Blue- Hypnotic and trance

Teal Blue- Soothing

Turquoise- Humor

Grey- Doubt

Charcoal Grey- Somber

Emerald Green – Intuitive Awareness

Forest Green- Prosperity and Abundance

Apple Green- Growth

Red- Passion and the color of fire. It is a high-energy color that invokes joy, happiness, enthusiasm, courage, virility, faith, and a vibrant life force.

Citrus Orange- Creative experience

Burnt Orange- Physical health

Peach- Biological Healing

Brown- Earth and Worry. Brown also represents the earth and soil and is the color of fertility.

Terracotta- Grounding

Lavender- Personal spirit, self-aware

Purple- Spiritual and esoteric study

Lemon Yellow- Analysis

Butter Yellow- Abstract Intuition

Gold- Emotional healing and suggests power and wealth. It was used sparingly in oriental rugs and was usually reserved for rugs that were especially woven for royalty and rulers.

Silver- Personal Power

White- Etheric Wisdom. It is a pure color and is associated with purity of the heart, innocence, selflessness, cleanliness, and peace.

Black- Death and symbolizing doom and destruction. Rug weavers very rarely used to create complete patterns or even to create the rug field. When they douse black, it is typically to create outlines and borders to define a precise design.

Our brain cells carry our transmission of color to our senses. Besides seeing and sensing color, many people can hear color! Listed here are colors of the week according to Hindu traditions.

- **Sunday**– Hindus believe it is auspicious to wear Red on Sunday. People also offer red flowers to Surya or the Sun God. Many keep a fast on this day eating just one meal, before sunset.

- **Monday**– As per Hinduism, Monday's color is Yellow, though people who fast also wear White on this day. Lord Shiva is the deity associated with this day of the week, so people often offer White flowers to this God. Monday is also associated with the Moon and colors linked to it are silver, light gray or blue.

- **Tuesday**– Pink is the color linked with Tuesday. In Hindu culture, this day is associated with the Monkey God or Lord Hanuman and people who fast and pray to this Lord can also wear Red. The day is also linked with Mars-the angry planet-which can be appeased by wearing Pink.

- **Wednesday**– Green is the color of the day for Wednesday. Wednesday is associated with Lord Vitthal as well as Budha (not Buddha) which is the deity linked with Jupiter.

- **Thursday**– People wear Orange or Yellow on this day. As per Hindu culture, this day is the day of Lord Vishnu who is known to wear Yellow.

- **Friday**– Friday color is Blue (Sea green or aquamarine are also acceptable). The day is also associated with Goddess Shakti who prefers White. So, Hindus wear either color on these days.

- **Saturday**-Wear the color of the royalty-Purple though you can also wear black, indigo, mauve, or dark grey, all of which are associated with wrath of Shani (Saturn). People in Indian villages also visit Shani shrines and make offerings of black oil, black sesame seeds and donate black clothes.

When I worked in quality control in a fabric dyeing plant in Piraeus, Greece we dyed cotton fabrics for the garment industry. Often black was a color. One of the fascinating traditions was because of the religious tradition for the family of the deceased to wear black for a year, or in the case of spouses many years. So, if someone in the staff had a death in the family, they would bring the clothes in and put them in at the end of the cycle for the color black.

Weaving is one the oldest crafts around. Humans know about weaving since Paleolithic era. Flax weavings are found in Fayum, Egypt, dating from around 5000 BC and was flax, which was replaced by wool around 2000 BC. By the beginning of counting the time weaving was known in all the great civilizations. Early looms need one or two persons to work on them. Bible refers to loom and weaving in many places.

Horizontal and vertical looms could be found in Asia, Africa, and Europe around 700AD. At that time also appeared pit-treadle loom with pedals for operating heddles which first appeared in Syria, Iran, and Islamic parts of East Africa.

Faithful were required by Islam to be covered from neck to ankle which increased the demand for cloth. In Africa, the rich wore cotton clothing while the poorer had to wear wool.

By 1177, loom was improved in Moorish Spain with rising higher above the ground on a stronger frame. Now the weaver's hands were free to pass the shuttle, while operating the heddles was done by the feet and became the standard European loom. In Medieval Europe, weaving was done at home and sold at fairs. The craft spread and the guilds were established. Wars, famine, and plague shifted manufacturing of fabrics from home to purpose-built centralized buildings.

Cotton is a plant that grows anywhere the temperature is hot, the growing season is long and there is much rain and irrigation. Ideal temperature must not go lower than 70degrees. In the USA cotton is grown from southern Virginia to central California. The USA brings to market approximately 18% of the world's production. Other major producers are China, India, Eastern Europe, Pakistan, Turkey, and Brazil.

For each plant the flowers are called a bill with each having up to 7or 8 seeds. Each seed may contain 20,000 fibers growing from its surface. These are then separated the fibers from the seeds and then pressed into a bale. Cotton breeders have done the same as those with animals: selected breeding to produce stronger and longer fibers and some are insect and stress tolerant.

New methods of bioengineered cottons have incorporated some polyester into the cotton fibers. The major breeds in cotton are upland, Pima, sea island and Egyptian and Gossypium. The grading of cotton is still done by hand. By itself, cotton can be washed with detergents and isn't as temperature sensitive as wool.

Caution must be taken that though it is a resilient fiber, it is subject to abrasions and structural weakening if treated too harshly. Though most handmade rugs are wool and many with cotton foundations the popularity of cotton dhurries one must be mindful of the fiber's integrity. So, the more you know about rugs the more you love them! I became fascinated with some of the untold stories in weaving. One area is just now becoming popular internationally for its weaving.

CHAPTER 7

WEAVERS OF NORTH AFRICA

North African carpets are those that originate from Morocco, Tunisia, and Egypt. They are usually identified by the tribe that creates them, not a town, as they are still nomadic. Morocco has been called a tapestry of cultures. Its culture has been influenced by native Berbers, expanding Arabs, missionary Europeans, and travelling Jews. The colors, sounds, and tastes of Morocco are more visible than in their arts. One of the most respected Moroccan art forms is textiles, fabrics and cloths that are ornately decorated and superbly designed. Moroccan culture may be a tapestry of cultures, and so are their textiles. Morocco's textile heritage is long reaching, dating back hundreds of years. African Berbers had their own forms of textiles, which over time were heavily and would continually practice. Across history, control over this important industry gave women a degree of economic and social power, something they were often otherwise denied. Throughout adolescence, women be expected to produce several pieces for various occasions to demonstrate their education and maturity. Once married, these women would produce textiles for their home and engage with other women to share techniques, styles, and ideas. To this day, textiles are primarily a women's art form in Morocco and still just as highly respected. In terms of the designs themselves, Moroccan women tend to favor geometric and abstract patterns. These patterns are chosen for their aesthetic values of symmetry and harmony rather than direct representation of earthly objects and ideas. Deep meaning is found in their patterns.

Embroidered textiles are found across all aspects of Moroccan life, from walls to floors to bags to clothes. Babies are swaddled in embroidered cloths, families are clothed in embroidered fabrics, and the dead are covered in embroidered shrouds. The history of Morocco's designs is tied to the experiences and cultures of the women who inhabit domestic spaces. These women came from many different lifestyles, mixing arts like henna painting and calligraphy into the fabrics that were eternally present in their daily lives. This is the rich past translates into the relationship between women, their surroundings, and their art forms. I read this statement and thought about all the arts and crafts from there and thought it summed it up so well!

Everything in Moroccan society was embroidered, including men !

Within various segments of Moroccan society, different patterns emerge as well. For example, stars are much more common amongst Jewish embroiderers. Azemmour embroideries are largely created by Jewish women of European ancestry, particularly Spanish or Portuguese and embrace European stitching patterns. Communities with ancestral ties to Algeria employed a Turkish style used to create a cloth called a *tensifa*.

Decoration and design of domestic textiles in traditional Moroccan culture since the early ages of trade with African, Middle Eastern and European countries is tied to its many influences of religion and culture that have grown within its borders. Moroccan textiles bridge the urban and rural spheres and is an art form practiced by women.

Embroidery, or the decoration of a textile (or leather) with needle and thread, was the "only pastime of the upper middle-class women" in Moroccan cities who used in their embroidery natural fine silk floss dyed in shimmering colors, derived from both animal and vegetal sources. These women learned to embroider textiles at a young age, and as they grew up used the skills, they developed to decorate their marriage trousseaus, or the personal possessions of a bride usually including clothes, accessories, and household linens and wares and even if they became one of many wives.

Maghreb Magic

Time has passed and I have healed.

But the magic and the melodies of the Maghreb have been woven into my story.

They have weavers there: Morocco, Egypt, Tunisia, Algeria each alive with its own haunting flavor.

Spells and spices, the beat of the drum, camels and cackling calls, souks and assassins, mosques and magicians are entwined in the culture.

The people of the desert know the power of the wind and have knowledge of the sands. Tribal wars and glories before we were even an idea here in the land of the free.

They come here and some swim in our melting pot and others cannot break themselves free from the dark chains of history, dripping with blood and buried in the sand.

The Beni Ourain Moroccan "tribe" is made up of 17 different Berber tribes that live in the Atlas Mountains. We see that natural dyes were used exclusively in Morocco until the mid to late 20th century which included henna, almond leaves, indigo, iron sulfate. This makes them sought after by the top interior designers who love them and look to feature them as rugs décor. The Atlas mountains are located in the region that borders Morocco, Algeria, and Tunisia. East–West direction is the pattern of movement. Atlas Mountain transportation routes are strongholds of ancient traditionalism as their isolation gave them their strength.

Women, for the most part, weave the rugs. Their design elements from their personal experience are translated into the carpet's designs. Usually, the design was created as references to natural events and aspects of daily life such as birth, fertility, nature, femininity, rural life, beliefs, and their spirituality.

Beni Ourain rugs from a special sheep in the Atlas Mountains that are a smaller sheep of an ancient breed. They produce the excellent high-quality wool that makes Beni Ourain rugs unique and of distinct quality. This breed still roams the rugged Middle Atlas Mountains in Morocco. Rugs have been woven by the indigenous people of Morocco since the Old Stone Age. Moroccan rugs have been woven by tribal peoples for their utility rather than for decorative purposes. Twentieth-century Moroccan rugs are widely collected in the West, and are almost always woven by tribes' people whose craft is passed down through the generations, which make them both a piece of history and a work of art.

Rug weaving in Libya

My quest in discovering more about rug weaving brought the Berbers to my attention. As in some of the other more familiar nomadic rug weavers, the Berbers are in a few of the North African countries. I had little or no knowledge about this part of the world until I came to San Diego. While having coffee in the first weeks I was here I met a graduate student from Jordan. His father was in the military and his mother was from a Berber tribe. I was fascinated, as he was studying history and politics and I realized so much of my education about this part of the world was very much a mystery, so I asked many questions! I wanted to know about the weaving of Berbers everywhere even in Libya. Most Berbers are—and have been throughout recorded history—sedentary agriculturalists.

Some Berbers practice forms of semi nomadism, or transhumance, during part of the year to maintain their flocks especially in the Aurès mountains and the southern part of the Middle Atlas. Sedentary Berbers typically live-in villages and eke out a meager peasant existence from small, irrigated gardens, and small flocks. In today's world, it is necessary for many of the most able-bodied men to export, their most marketable asset, their labor. Many villages are largely devoid of men between the ages of sixteen and forty. They emigrate temporarily, usually without families, both to North African cities and to European industrial centers and, from there, send home the money that, by living frugally, they can accumulate. Without their support, these villages and areas simply could not survive. Berber artistic expression is linked to utilitarian object such as pottery, architecture, and jewelry.

All are characterized by predominantly geometrical, nonrepresentational patterns. Neither the forms and patterns nor the techniques appear to have changed significantly since ancient times, and they can be related directly to forms from way back in the Iron Age in the Mediterranean basin. While they are not especially original or exclusive to Berbers, one is struck by the extraordinary persistence and continuity, in Berber country, of the tradition.

Berber languages are generally only spoken, seldom written. Among the Tuareg, however, there subsists an alphabet, the *tifinagh,* which descends from the Libyan alphabet that is found in ancient inscriptions throughout much of North Africa and now in present-day Tunisia and eastern Algeria. This alphabet, which like Arabic is essentially consonantal, can be written right to left or left to right, occasionally vertically.

Among the Tuareg, it is used primarily for short inscriptions on rocks and for brief messages but does not seem to be employed for the recording of stories, documents, or history, those uses for which writing is basic in our Western cultures. Some efforts have been made by advocates of Berber cultural affirmation, to adapt the *tifinagh* to such functions and to broaden its use to other Berber-speaking groups, as in Kabylia and in Morocco. There has been only very limited success and those publications in Algeria and in Morocco to help explain written in the Berber language generally use the Latin-based transcription system employed by the French.

I once had a guide to Tunisian from the Peace Corps. With the nomadic lifestyle and many influences, the languages in this region are worth a book of their own. Berber literature is then essentially oral. It includes many traditional stories—tales of animals, marvelous tales with ogres and monsters, tales of kings and princesses and legends, and a myriad other stories that hand down the moral and ethical base of Berber society. As for poetry, among the Berbers it goes with music and is—unlike the tales and stories—constantly regenerated around a wide spectrum of subjects. Traditional forms, such as the often-bantering repartee in the context of celebratory line dances in Morocco. There are more lyrical forms, songs of the heart and its joys and pains. There are the elaborate and often quite lengthy commentaries by troubadour-like itinerant singers who hold forth, often quite bitingly, on all subjects, including the political scene.

One cannot fail to mention Berber popular music, which constitutes the richest and most fertile field of Berber literary expression today. Of the languages with which Berber has shared North Africa at different times and places—among them Phoenician, Latin, Germanic (German and English), Turkish, Italian, Spanish, and French—none has had the profound effect that the Arabic dialects have had.

Most Berber languages have a high percentage of borrowing from Arabic, as well as from other languages. Least influenced are the Tuareg languages; most influenced, those that are near urban centers and from whose areas there has traditionally been much temporary emigration for work.

Berber languages survive because children learn their first language from their mothers and it continues to be the language of the home, of the private world, long after they become adults and the men become bilingual. Berber women continue, in most areas, to have little education and little contact with the Arabic-speaking world around them, so their children will doubtless continue to learn and to perpetuate Berber languages. The movements to preserve Berber culture, most developed in Kabylia and somewhat in Morocco, will also doubtless have a conservative effect. Where Berber is spoken only in a village or two surrounded by Arabic speakers, it is disappearing. In the larger Berber-speaking regions, however, it is quite resistant, and the numbers of speakers are growing at nearly the same rate as that at which the population increases.

Berber languages and cultures have been neglected and even repressed by the agencies of the central governments. This need to discourage cultural differences in the building of the nation-state—cultural differences that, it was felt, had been exploited by the French colonial regimes to divide the colonized and impose their authority. In both Algeria and Morocco, there exist official political parties made up essentially of Berbers, with Berber cultural preservation as one of their highest priorities.

CHAPTER 8

PATTERNS

Pattern

Rugs hold a pattern.

Within: I feel the story!

To repair these works of love is simple.

If you approach with love.

Their story is revealed. What wonderful colors!

Each a story, they understand the pattern,

Each a history: Anything is possible. All it takes is love.

I have always loved patterns. I got in the habit of looking into the coffee grounds of Turkish style cups. If you have ever had coffee in Greece, Turkey, or the Middle east you understand that coffee is ground to a fine powder and is boiled with water and sugar. A dear friend had a coffee shop in the old Monstiraki district in Athens. This blend is boiled in a copper pot over hot coals. Once you sip the coffee, the grounds leave a pattern. You can see the future! I would occasionally do this at the Greek restaurant I worked at when I first arrived. On one occasion I shared what I saw with people I never met; they were stunned at how much I shared that was true! Over time I have expanded this to trying to see the larger patterns in our daily lives. I have one of those pots, gifted to me at a festival. I was selling olive oil; my neighbors were Turkish selling jewelry and metal wares. It made me smile to think here we are thousands of miles away, being neighbors.

The importance of symbology in rug designs is deep and fascinating subject. We have explored some of the ancient eastern figures and symbols and now you are ready to explore with me some of the most fascinating designs: the ones in Persian rugs.

So, let's begin with one of the most controversial, the latch hook which is also, a variation of the swastika and has the same meaning. The swastika is derived from the Sanskrit word Svasti, or presence. It dates to around three or four thousand BC. This symbol has been found in nearly all excavations of prehistoric times and relics of primitive people all over the world. It has been found in the history of the people from Ancient Greece, Egyptians, Chinese, Japanese, East Indians, Aztecs, mound builders and the Indians of North and South America with all who share a common meaning of good luck and happiness. The latch hook has been called the trademark of Caucasian Rugs in which it is used consistently. It is apparent in nearly all Western Asian designs.

With the Chinese the latch hook is for privacy. It takes many forms and is also found extensively in Turkish, Caucasian, and Turkmen product. Four of the latch hook designs interlocked in a clockwise pattern with the cross at right angles, interlocking like a t shaped form it will make a border design that is found in the decorations of Samarkand and Chinese rugs. This symbol in India is drawn below the seats intended for bridegrooms as well as beneath the plates containing food to be offered to the gods and is tattooed on the arms. It is also drawn on the scalp at thread ceremony and on the bottom of the feet at all important ceremonies, such as marriages and the like.

There are weavers in the isthmus that create the Antique Caucasian rugs between the Black sea and the Caspian sea. Very bold in design and color than the Turkish; possibly the mountain forms and the strong contrasts of snow and earth are reflected in them. Native designs have been unaffected by foreign influences. Practically all the patterns are geometric. The Ghiordes knot, wool warp and woof, and the prayer-rug size are characteristics of these rugs. There is almost no variation in the six colors that are used, but fortunately for the achievement of harmony, some one color always predominates in these rug and carpet. There are many directions to take this story. When I think about early civilizations, my mother the History and Geography teacher's lessons about Mesopotamia between the Tigris and the Euphrates always come to mind.

The people were known for their textiles, pottery, and metals. The name came from the Greek word meaning the land between two rivers. Abundantly rich soil, much commerce began here. The earliest known system of writing was invented here. Gilgamesh and the Code of Hammurabi began here. The people of the Sumerian states spoke Akkadian a Semitic language. Their architecture known as a ziggurat, a pyramid type of building. It makes me smile to know at present I work next to a modern-day pyramid of glass.

CHAPTER 9

COOL OLD RUGS

One of the oldest cities has been the home of very cool rugs. At times Samarkand has been one of the greatest cities of Central Asia in the past. Located on the Silk Road on the way to China. Samarkand is in Uzbekistan. The city is noted for being an Islamic center for scholarly study. In the 14th century, the city of Samarkand became the capital of the empire of Timor (also known as Tamerlane). The city has carefully preserved the traditions of ancient crafts: embroidery, gold embroidery, silk weaving, engraving on copper, ceramics, carving and painting on wood. I have always found this city extremely fascinating as it was truly the beginning of crossing cultures to do commerce. Chinese Buddhist symbols represents the crossroads at Samarkand and that is why it is a popular symbol in the rugs.

Human activity in the city from the late Paleolithic era, though there is no direct evidence of when exactly Samarkand was founded, some theories are that it was founded between the 8th and 7th centuries BC. By the time of the Achaemenid dynasty of Persia, it was the capital of the Sogdian satrapy. The city it was known by its Greek name of Marakanda when Alexander the Great was its ruler. The city was ruled by a succession of Iranian, Persian, and Turkish peoples. Samarkand in 1220 was taken over by Genghis Khan. In 2001 it became one of UNESCO's heritage sites: Samarkand a Cross Road of Cultures. Archeological excavations held within the city limits as well as suburban areas unearthed evidence of human activity as early as 40,000 years old, which is late paleolithic era. A group of Mesolithic era (12-7 millennium BCE) archeological sites were discovered on the outskirts of the city). They found canals, supplying with water the city and its suburbs appeared around the 7th to 5th centuries BCE (early Iron Age). There is no direct evidence of when exactly Samarkand was founded. Researchers of Institute of Archeology of Samarkand set existence of the city between the 8th and 7th centuries BCE.

Samarkand has been one of the main centers of Sogdian civilization from its early days. By the time of the Achaemenid dynasty of Persia, it had become the capital of the Sogdian satrapy. Samarkand was a diverse religious community and was home to a number of many religions that include Judaism, Christianity, Buddhism, Hinduism, Zoroastrianism, Nestorian Christianity, and even Manichaeism. The city has continued to be synonymous with the crossroads of culture.

The legend says that during the Persian Abbasid rule, there were two Chinese prisoners from the battle of Talas in 751 who taught them the secret of papermaking. This began the first paper mill in the Islamic world and this invention spread throughout the east and from there to Europe.

The 10th-century Iranian author Istakhri, who travelled in Transoxiana, provides a vivid description of the natural riches of the region he calls "Smarkandian Sogd":I know no place in it or in Samarkand itself where if one ascends some elevated ground one does not see greenery and a pleasant place, and nowhere near it are mountains lacking in trees .Every town and settlement have a fortress...It is the most fruitful of all the countries of God in it are the best trees and fruits, in every home are gardens, cisterns and flowing water. Marco Polo records his journey along the Silk Road, describes Samarkand as "a very large and splendid city".

Timur's commitment to the arts is evident in the way he was ruthless with his enemies but merciful towards those with special artistic abilities. He spared the lives of artists, craftsmen, and architects so that he could bring them to improve and beautify his capital. The color of the buildings in Samarkand also has significant meaning behind it. For instance, blue is the most common and dominant color that will be found on the buildings, which was used by Timur to symbolize a large range of ideas. For one, the blue shades seen in the Gur-i Amir are colors of mourning.

Blue was the color of mourning in Central Asia at the time, as it is in many cultures even today, and its dominance in the city's mausoleum appears to be a very rational idea. In addition, blue was also seen as the color that would ward off "the evil eye" in Central Asia and the notion is evident in the number of doors in and around the city that were colored blue during this time. Furthermore, blue was representative of water, which was a particularly rare resource around the Middle East and Central Asia; coloring the walls blue symbolized the wealth of the city.

CHAPTER 10

RUG WEAVING REGIONS

The term "Oriental rug" refers to any hand-knotted rug created in the ancient rug-weaving centers of the Near East and Far East: from the Balkans through Turkey, North Africa, the Caucasus, Iran, Afghanistan, Pakistan, India, China, and Nepal.

While the exact origin of hand-woven oriental rugs is uncertain, ancient writings mention a variety of weavings and locations. The earliest surviving piece–known as the Pazyryk carpet–dates to 400-500 BC. (Discovered in a burial site excavated in southern Siberia between 1947-49, it is now part of the Hermitage Museum Collection in Leningrad.) Certain scholars, in fact, believe that Oriental rugs probably existed even before the building of the Egyptian Pyramids and the fabled palaces of Babylon.

CHAPTER 11

VALUING A RUG

- • ✘ • **Knot Density**
- • ✘ • **Materials Used**
- • ✘ • **Design Elements**
- • ✘ • **Colors, Blending, and Dye types**
- • ✘ • **Age**
- • ✘ • **Condition of rug**
- • ✘ • **Demand & Availability**

These are the factors that weigh in how rug prices are determined between the buyer and the seller at both the production, wholesale, and retail level. Even the most knowledgeable oriental rug broker in the world will say to you that oriental rugs are still subjective to what the people "WANT" at a particular time. What is popular has the most effect on the current price of a particular oriental rug. The question poised for the smart buyer is, "Is this rug worth the price being asked"? What is "in fashion" demands prices well beyond reasonable valuations and are often subject to sharp downturns in price.

Knot Density

Knot count is based on taking the number of knots/nodes and counting one inch in each direction, and then multiplying these two figures together. Looking at the back of a rug, first make sure that you can find one node color by itself. If two colored nodes are always together, then you have an oriental rug that is not fully depressed, and you are seeing both sides of the knot. This means your figure must be divided by two, to get the actual knot count.

It is best to do this counting in a few places on the rug to get an average count. It's not easy but helps to give you a greater appreciation for the weavers. Here is one method of valuing a rug based on the quality of the weave.

Knot Density	Table Points
675 and above	10
575 to 674	9
425 to 574	8
320 to 424	7
245 to 319	6
180 to 244	5
140 to 179	4
90 to 139	3
64 to 89	2
37 to 64	1
0 to 36	0

Materials Used	Points
Silk on silk	10
Kurk Wool on silk/fine cotton	9
Fine wool w/wo silk inlay on cotton	8
Good wool " "	7
Standard Shanghai wool on cotton	6
Standard wool on wool	5
Mercerized cotton/ low quality wool	4
Dead wool on cotton	3
Dead wool on wool	2
Dead wool on jute	1
Cotton on jute	0

Design Elements

Points

10 points - Minutely detailed curvilinear patterns cover the entire background.

8 points - Minutely detailed rectilinear patterns, or fine curvilinear throughout.

7 points - Picture/portrait rugs, moderately floral curvilinear designs w/without a medallion, fine Turkoman (Bokhara)

5 points - Moderate angles/curves, allover designs, open areas

4 points - Less detailed rectilinear/curvilinear designs like Heriz, and open-field Kirman.

3 points - Simple and/or repeating patterns like Turkomans with large guls, often called (elephant footprints).

2 points- Carved Chinese 120L or above.

1 point - Carved Chinese less than 120L, Indo Aubusson/Savonnerie.

0 points - One color rug carved, plain rug.

Colors, Blending, and Dye types

<u>Points</u>

10 points - (15) or more colors and shades blended in perfect harmony.

Rug may be either Jewel or Antique tones. Top quality vegetable or Chrome dyes.

8 points - (10) or more colors and shades blended in perfect harmony.

Not quite the "WOW" feeling. More Chrome dyes being used.

6 points - (6) or more colors that blend well. No single color jumps out at you. Most modern quality production falls into this category.

4 points - (4) or more colors that blend. Nothing knocks your socks off here. Middle quality Kirman, Turkoman, Kurdish, Heriz, and the like.

2 points - (4) or more colors with the insertion of a color that just does not quite fit the blend. Many tribal oriental rugs fall into this category using a "hot, or electric" color.

1 point - (3) or more "hot or electric" colors that do not blend, rugs with a bad antique wash, and rugs that have been overly toned down.

0 points - Oriental rugs with colors beyond help, even with chemical washing. Includes single- and two-toned rugs.

Age

<u>Points</u>

10 points - 100 years and older (antique)

8 points - 70 years and older (semi-antique)

6 points - 50 years and older (old)

4 points - 30 years and older

2 points - 20 years and older

1 point - Below 20 years

0 points - Below 10 years (considered new)

Condition of a Rug

<u>Points</u>

10 points - Oriental rug is "like new". The rugs entire pile is present, including the fringe, side cords, and selvedges. There is no damage to this rug. Antique, and semi-antique rugs a rarely found in this condition.

9 points - Only fringe shows some wear, and pile is even throughout. The other conditions of the rug remain perfect.

8 points - The rug pile is worn evenly and reduced in height about 1/4th of an inch. There may be a few professional repairs not apparent under normal examination.

7 points - This oriental rug is still in excellent condition despite the past owners not washing the rug for many years, if at all. This happens to many rugs. The wash will significantly raise the value or lower the ending value.

5 points - Rugs in this group have an even pile height slightly above a 1/4 inch. There may be some minor repairs needed. End-stopping may have taken away some of the sub borders or border guards.

4 points - Pile of rug remains even and between 1/8th and 1/4th of an inch. No stains are present, that cannot be removed.

3 points - Pile less than 1/8th inch high. Foundation is starting to show in several places. No serious stains are present. The oriental rug may be restored at considerable expense. The rug may not be placed in a high traffic area.

1 point - This rug needs major repairs. Part of the ends or sides of the rug are lost. Stains are permanent. Major re-knotting may be needed.

0 points - Rug is cracking. or is beyond repair, to return any kind of value. This situation comes at you more quickly the lower the quality of rug.

Demand & Availability

Points

10 points - Rare antique oriental rug

8 points - Semi-rare antique oriental rug

7 points - Old rug not being produced in any real quantity

6 points - Old rug still produced, and specialized "reproductions" of antiques

5 points - New high quality oriental rug not being produced in any real quantity

4 points - High quality rugs still being produced

3 points - Good quality rugs still being produced

2 points - Average quality rugs being produced

1 point - Bazaar quality rugs being produced

0 points - Low-end mass-produced rugs

Dealers may charge much more, or less for any rug. That is their option, your option to be informed an educated on such when you purchase. Oriental rugs are commodities subject to supply and demand. Oriental Rug Brokers are always knowing these changes in supply, demand, and associated price. The retail buyer is not. This formula is guideline for determining rug quality and value, If you want to know general retail prices right at this moment, you have two choices. Long shipping times, remote regions, and political unrest, all contribute to this market volatility.

It is very expensive for a retailer to place millions of dollars of oriental rug inventory on the floor. Retailers pay rent, insurance, utilities, advertising, employees, benefits, transportation, and numerous other monthly items. Retailers should be allowed to charge a reasonable profit to cover these expenses. If you are paying substantially less than average retail, **there is a reason!**

Magical Mysteries

Glowing fibers

Dancing patterns

Fantasies holding history

Stories of the world

Displayed in perfect symmetry

Designs that delight

With magical mysteries

A world to be discovered again

How it conceals itself

From the untrained eye

Though fully accessible

To those who understand

The brilliance, the beauty,

The love.

⚉⚉⚉

CHAPTER 12

RUGS FROM CHINA

I once again had a discussion with a client. Her parents had bought one when they were working overseas. Now 30 years later shouldn't it be worth more? The biggest problem is that if you don't understand world politics, rug pricing can be a mystery. Since the world began, weaving has been going on. The popular weaving centers with the finest craftsmen have followed where the best materials and great workshops are located. For example, over 100 years ago Kashan silks were the finest. Now when you say fine 100% silk you think Qum or perhaps Hereke. Carpets woven in towns and regional centers like Tabriz, Kerman, Mashhad, Kashan, Isfahan, Nain, and Qom are characterized by their designs. The measure of the best rugs is the Persian standard.

Places where rugs are made are known as the "Rug Belt", which stretches from Morocco across North Africa, the Middle East, and into Central Asia and northern India. Most of Asia has weaving, especially the countries of Turkey, Tibet, China, Iran, throughout the Caucasus and Pakistan, Afghanistan and India. It is hard to imagine that rugs were made in South Africa in the 1980's and 1990's. Somewhere in 2007 I worked for a business that had furniture and rugs. A few were from that region! It's really amazing that knowing rugs has opened many doors for me. It makes other rug enthusiasts connect immediately as if we do speak that unspoken language.

People from different cultures, countries, racial groups, and religious faiths are involved in the production of oriental rugs. The events of history shaped the industry. During the first embargo, China and India stepped in to fill the market void. Since they were some of the only handmade rugs available, they were priced for what the market could handle. Now the same rugs sell for like a tenth of the price so when you get an appraisal, it based on current market value wholesale and retail and a bit about the history of the rug. Like we spoke about in the section of valuing a rug. Is it a known designer? Is it one of a kind? Is it signed? Did it belong to someone famous? What condition is it in? The client I spoke to had it washed and put it on social media. If not, they would keep it. It was one of those dense pastel-colored carved rugs! On the other hand, a client has a Fette Li and I have located another one for her new home and though not as pricey, they keep a reasonable value.

So, remember the rug market has followed the world.

There are rugs made before the Persian Revolution (1978-1999) India and China filled the gap. Then there are rugs after the revolution (1999-2009) we see the growth in Persian rug export. The embargo time (2009-2016) Pakistan and Afghanistan took up the slack. The American presence in Afghanistan (2001-?) had a profound impact on the world. The events after September 11 created a focus on that region.

The increased amount of people going to the region created a great market for foreigners buying rugs production increased. Due to travel costs, import taxes etc. the past few years has seen an increase in North African rugs. So, when trying to value a rug you must evaluate the story and the history.

Chinese rugs are easily identified compared to traditional Persian rugs, due to the unique characteristics found in Chinese rugs. The Chinese rug-making history is somewhat ambiguous, without a clear idea of who influenced the origins of rug making in the Far East. What is known is that traditional rug weaving was first found in China in the Northwest territories as early as the 500s and the designs were largely influenced by Buddhist and Taoist symbols. The rich Chinese culture is depicted in their weaving, and unlike the traditional Persian rug, the symbols and colors all have specific meanings and intents. In the late 1800s a monk from the Northwest territories of China moved to Peking (Beijing) and set up rug weaving schools to help the poor earn an income. The weaving style was much like what was being done in the Northwest, utilizing the same symbols and designs. These factories were successful and started producing the first Peking rugs. The 1920s and 1930s saw a slight change in the production of Chinese rugs to include more "art deco" designs to appeal to the Western market. The introduction of this design and its success in the Western market saw the decline of the Peking rugs. Because rug weaving in Peking began to employ its citizens, it was more important to the Chinese to keep working then to limit production and increase profits, therefore an abundance of Peking rugs was available in a short time.

Peking rugs have their own identifying characteristics that make them unique, even among other Chinese rugs. The colors most often used are blues, tans, and ivories. The design is an open field with various pictures placed throughout the field. The images are often independent of each other -- seemingly floating throughout the field. Peking rugs tend to be tightly woven, low pile with high quality wool -- compared to more modern Chinese productions that are more coarsely woven with thicker pile.

Some of the most common pictures depicted in Chinese rugs include bats, lotus flowers, butterflies, dragons, and fish...all of which have specific meanings. There is a symbol called the Shoo and is one of the most common images seen in Peking rugs. This symbolizes long life. Other symbols include:

Bats -- good luck

Butterflies -- happy marriage

Dragons – power

Peony – wealth

Lotus -- purity

The carpet weaver has grown as a creator weaving poetry of myriad designs, with every knot they tie. A carpet weaver's skills are their own and the design evolves are from his mind to be translated into beautiful form with the help of wool and silks. Indian carpet industry draws inspiration from countries as diverse as Persia, China, Afghanistan in weaving intricate pieces of high artistic value. The specialty of Indian carpets lies in its exquisite designs with natural and traditional motifs, subtle elegance, attractive color combinations and excellent workmanship. Indian carpet industry has travelled a long distance since the time Akbar introduced carpet weaving in India. They are mainly exported to USA, Canada, Spain, Turkey, Mexico, Australia, South Africa, Belgium, Holland, New Zealand, Denmark, and many other European countries.

The industry, vibrant since the mid-nineteenth century had to face rough weathers during the World Wars I & II and the Great Depression of the 1930's due to recession and a slump in demand. Between 1947 and 1965, carpet exports ranged from INR 32.2 million to INR 56.6 million

Student of Life

I came to learn the things

That ancient ruins didn't know

Masters of other cultures

Persia, Tibet, Mecca, China

As though the universe unfolds for me personally

I understand Rumi,

About being drunk with knowledge!

It's the poet's blessing

And his curse

That the worlds reveal themselves quite clearly

Waiting to be correctly interpreted

And translated so that

All may know its wonder.

Art Deco refers to the style launched at the 1925 Paris World's Fair Exhibition of Modern and Industrial Decorative Art. Art Deco rugs introduced a new, nonrestrictive color palette. Bright, never-before-used combinations were the new trend. The soft blue of traditional Chinese rugs was replaced by a more vibrant lapis blue, while the traditional calm gold gave way to varying shades of ochre, green, raspberry, plum, purple, and teal also became popular.

Because of its low production costs, China became the hub for weaving Art Deco rugs exported to the States. There were hundreds of factories producing rugs, but it was two enterprising Americans who dominated: Helen Fette and Walter Nichols. Little did they know their names would become synonymous with the term and virtually all rugs woven during that era, which ran from the mid 1920's to around 1935. Helen Fette went to China as a missionary, selling small rugs to raise funds for charities. She teamed up with Chinese rug manufacturer Li Meng Shu to form the Fette-Li Company. They started producing rugs out of the Peking area in the early 1920's and were one of the largest exporters of the period.

In 1924 Walter Nichols opened the doors of his venture, Nichols Super Yarn and Carpets in Tientsin, North China. Super Yarn because of the machine spun yarn, the strong cotton used for the foundation, and the overall tightly packed weave of the rugs. In stark contrast to his Fette counterpart, a Nichols rug was quite dense and heavy. Both Fette and Nichols placed identifying fabric tags on the back of their rugs.

Nichols also stamped his name onto the backside of the fringe, however if the fringe has worn down or been repaired, the mark is usually absent. Because Fette and Nichols were so closely associated with the Deco period, rugs woven in their trademark style, absent any remaining identification marks, are routinely referred to as Fette or Nichols style. No other Oriental rugs are as representative of their time as the Chinese Decos. The dynamics of the designs and of experimentation with abstract forms and unrestrained colors.

CHAPTER 13

EUROPE

One of my most favorite parts of studying rugs is the symbolism, the unspoken language. Since a child looking for stories in the rocks on a beach on the Atlantic Ocean, looking for patterns absorbed many of my hours. Later as I got deep into rugs, I learned there was field of study devoted to this called Semiotics. It is explained as the theory of signs and symbols. It deals especially with their function in both artificially constructed and natural languages and comprises syntactics, semantics, and pragmatics. The universal symbols for red/hot and blue cold are a great example.

There is a class at Aarhus University in Denmark. If you didn't know there is a history of textiles in Scandinavia.

Scandinavia is known for its Rya and Rollakan rugs that date back to the 16th century. The region usually includes three countries in Northern Europe with a common cultural heritage: Norway, Sweden, and Denmark. Each of these places tends to have cold climates, long winters, and people who live in smaller homes in which neat and orderly interiors mean to focus on design without clutter. They love nature and strong craftsmanship traditions using natural materials. When we look at their textile design, this means creating and planning how fabrics look and feel and what a textile made of. It can be knitted or woven, and what type of texture you select.

This concept includes ideas about designs or patterns on a fabric surface, and whether they are woven into it or printed or dyed on its surface. The current design focus going towards mid-century modern decors has surely done wonders for the prices of Scandinavian rugs and they are finally being recognized for the great work of art that they truly are. Scandinavian Rugs can be found in both flat weaves as well as piled carpets.

A Swedish company, Ekelund Weavers has been around since 1692. Over 400 years, this family-owned business has produced woven fabrics of cotton and linen with traditional and contemporary patterns. Nature-inspired designs feature patterns with plants and animals that are clear and crisp, colorful forms against clean backgrounds that are not overly fussy or cluttered. All the textile items are practical things like towels, dishcloths, and table runners. Before the 19th century, however, plant textiles were mainly made from locally available raw materials, in Scandinavia, these were: nettle, hemp, and flax. It is generally believed that in Viking and early Middle Ages Scandinavia hemp was used only for coarse textiles (i.e., rope and sailcloth). Here we present an investigation of 10 Scandinavian plant fiber textiles from the Viking and Early Middle Ages, believed to be locally produced. Up till now, they were all believed to be made of flax. We show that 4 textiles, including two pieces of the famous Överhogdal Viking wall-hanging, are in fact made with hemp (in three cases hemp and flax are mixed). This indicates that hemp was important, not only for coarse but also for fine textile production in Viking and Early Middle Ages in Scandinavia.

The literature on Scandinavian Viking and Early Middle Ages, most fine plant fiber textile remains are referred to as flax without any mentioning of analytical tests. One of the few exceptions from this is Agnes Geijer, who in the 1930s investigated the textile finds from the Swedish Viking settlement Birka, near Lake Mälaren.

In the early 20th century, several Scandinavian women designers began to gain notice for their work. In 1873 - 1941, a Swedish weaver who became known for her rugs created designs that featured geometric and nature-inspired shapes with colors that reflected the light and hues of summer. Mass-Fjetterström started her own weaving workshop in 1919 and became highly collectible. Her carpets are usually more modern. This has created a surge in value as well as the massive increase in demand seems to be here to stay. For centuries, the Scandinavian people wove rugs out of necessity. The frigid winters and driving snows have always made the region particularly inhospitable, especially by European standards. For instance, tulips were the flower of choice for Scandinavians. Therefore, the tulip motifs became a staple in Scandinavian rugs. Local animals and birds also made their way into these new designs – creating an intriguing synthesis of Eastern and Western aesthetic preferences. When the Rya rug style fist came into its own as a distinct style of weaving, they were generally woven to be used as blankets or cloaks. The passing down Ryas between parents and their children began the Scandinavian tradition of the wedding rug. That said, perhaps the inverse is true. Regardless, during the middle and late seventeenth century, it was a tradition for marrying couples to have rugs made specially to commemorate their union.

These dowry rugs would usually incorporate the initials of the bride and groom, the date of the weddings, and imaginative representations of the couple. Countries that had had limited trade with one another were suddenly trading commercial goods on a scale never seen. As such, the average consumers were suddenly exposed to certain items which they had previously could not afford. This phenomenon had an especially significant impact on the rug industry in Norway.

Initially utilitarian and made in muted solid colors – often blacks, grays, whites, and yellows – Scandinavian rugs would later feature geometric constructions and floral motifs inspired by the aesthetics of Oriental rugs. It was beginning in the mid-17th century that new elements began to appear in Scandinavian rugs — the tree of life design, floral patterns (with an emphasis on tulips), and depictions of birds and animals were introduced into the design of these rugs, bringing exotic appeal and new beauty to traditional pieces. Modern-day rugs in Scandinavia are from these brands: Scandinavian brands, including Marimekko, Almedahls, Vallila Interior, and Nordic Nest.

Because of my interest in this class in Denmark, I realized the ability to remember what a certain type of rugs and identify them have much to do with visual learning. Visual Learners can utilize graphs, charts, maps, diagrams, and other forms of visual stimulation to effectively interpret information.

Chapter 14

THE SILK ROAD

Are you one of those people who closes your eyes to envision the exact location of where you left your car keys? Do you bring up mental imagery when you're trying to remember what you did last Tuesday afternoon? Do you remember the cover of every book you've ever read? Do you have a photographic or near-photographic memory? Perhaps you are one of those people with the visual learning style. This means that people need to *see* information to learn it, and this "seeing" takes many forms from spatial awareness, photographic memory, color/tone, brightness/contrast, and other visual information. The teachers use overheads, the chalkboard, pictures, graphs, maps, and many other visual items to entice a visual learner into knowledge.

Some traits of visual learners easily visualize objects, great sense of balance, an excellent organizer, very color-oriented, they can see the passage from a page in a book in his or her mind. One tends to see minute similarities and differences between objects and people easily, thus identifying rugs.

When we talk about rugs, we usually mean Persian or "Oriental "rugs we typically refer to those woven in the Persian Empire of old. There is much reference to the "Silk Road". Silk has always been an expensive and desirable commodity; it was brought from distant lands and required highly specialized and laborious techniques of processing, spinning, dyeing, and weaving; it feels sensuous against the skin but is very durable and can be woven with the most intricate patterns, rendered in brilliant jewel-like colors. Its trade routes and markets were zealously guarded and fought over, since whoever controlled its commercial activities and industrial centers reaped significant financial benefits. The Ottoman Empire was strategically located on the path of the east-west silk route bridging Asia and Europe. Silk, transported by caravans from Iran passed through Anatolia as far as Bursa, Where Europeans, mostly Italians, purchased the goods. Bursa was the major center for the international silk trade during the early sixteenth century and provided substantial revenues to the state by customs, taxes and brokerage fees levied from the Iranian and Italian merchants; in addition, it developed its own textile industry. Most of the raw silk that arrived in Bursa was sold to Europeans, but some was reserved for domestic use. In 1988, on my first trip to Turkey, we went on an excursion to a textile factory in Bursa. They made towels, and our gracious guides invited us to purchase. If then I understood the direction my life would take, I would have asked to see a carpet factory, though I did get to the Rug Bazaar! Although silk began to be produced in Bursa in the second half of the sixteenth century, its output was insufficient to supply the demand, and the Ottoman world continued to rely on imported raw material both for its domestic needs and resale. This is commonly referred to as the Silk Road. The protection of this lucrative trade of silk and rugs was of great interest to the sultans and was in part responsible for the wars with the Safavids throughout the sixteenth century.

So many of these poems were written while working in the rug gallery. It's as if the rugs were speaking to me in some way!

Speaking the Unspoken Language

Alive with color,

Rich in patterns, radiating my history. Tribal weavings

Speak the unspoken language of the soul. I know that language!

So many days the rugs have been calling me and teaching me, how to see beyond the words.

Worlds above the grid of humanity, beneath the layers of the earth, out in the depths of the sea.

Luring me into their story, I am an eager listener.

The ancient ways are the same across the globe.

Symbols are universal.

At one time we all knew these forms, which have been woven generations after generations.

Star seekers, dolphin divers, herders, and huntsmen. Ancient cultures still know.

We can speak. To each other across time, across the world.

If only more could remember how to speak.

The language which is unspoken.

In the language of weaving, words don't matter. We can watch hands move as they made intricate patterns with cotton and silk thread– these fibers. Every artisan and craftsperson there are a language unique to their craft. In weaving, one of the ways we communicate is through weaving drafts. One draft can communicate a multitude of things—from the threading and treadling sequences to sleying requirements and yarn size variations. Drafts can also overcome language barriers. One can see pattern books is a 100-year-old Russian weaving pattern book makes as much sense as one written today. The challenge in learning how to read drafts is the same learning a foreign language. The terms may seem unfamiliar at first, but with practice it begins to make more sense. Plus, there are even "dialects" to weaving drafts. This is especially true for historical drafts.

I understand that concept as my most treasured rug identification book was written in 1910! Since color photos were expensive, the author gave a detailed account of how to identify a rug in words and it nearly doubled my knowledge.

Rug World

Where do you most often find me? Rug world! The air is different, the rules are different. Step into the salon, a tradition thousands of centuries old. Rugs fly, tea is served. Cultures meet that understand the language of soul. The unspoken dialect of symbols and colors. Look into rug world. Imagine the caravans, feel the weavers, understand the reverence to spirit and traditions. Experience the beauty while indulging in its divinity. The air of practicality pervades as transactions are completed, tea and stories are shared. A word is worth a fortune in Rug World.

CHAPTER 15

PERSIAN RUGS

Most current tomes on rugs have very well documented sections on rugs from Iran. They are usually classified as "Persian" because of the extent that that weaving of the Persian Empire in its heyday encompassed most of the Silk Road and the Rug Belt. Persian carpets and rugs of various types were woven in parallel by nomadic tribes, in village and town workshops, and by royal court manufactories and tell the story of Iran. Court manufactories of the Safavid era are treasured in museums and private collections all over the world today because of their artistic beauty. Their patterns and designs have set an artistic tradition for court manufactories which was kept alive during the entire duration of the Persian Empire up to the last royal dynasty of Iran. Carpets woven in towns and regional centers. As centers of importance changed the top weaving cities changed as well. Kashan, Kerman, and Tabriz have been fantastic examples of city rugs. Rugs woven by the villages and various tribes of Iran are distinguished by their fine wool, bright and elaborate colors, and specific, traditional patterns. Nomadic and small village weavers like those of Gabbeh, or Bakhtiari, often produce rugs with bolder and sometimes more coarse designs, which are considered as the most authentic and traditional rugs of Persia, as opposed to the artistic, pre-planned designs of the larger workplaces.

Carpets and rugs have been regarded as objects of high artistic and utilitarian value and prestige since the first time they were mentioned by ancient Greek writers. Although the term "Persian carpet" most often refers to pile-woven textiles, flat-woven carpets like kilims, jajims, suzanis are also part of the rich and manifold tradition of Persian carpet weaving. In working in a business that imported rugs and sold retail and wholesale, there is much to be learned. I was fortunate to have been through the process of receiving the rugs after customs inspections and learning how identify and remember something unique and special of each piece.

Bales of rugs would arrive and opening each was like Christmas once again! Of course, part of being in a tourist area, we met rug lovers from all over the world. I have had fascinating conversations with diverse groups like Chinese rug wholesalers, individuals from a world spiritual convention, met some carpet designers from Armenia, to name a few. We also shipped purchased rugs worldwide, I remember fondly packing an Antique Persian rug to ship by air to Dubai, where it would match one the owners had already.

Timeless Tabriz

I awoke with a terrific realization

Every rug is a portal

To another world, another way of life

If they knew more people would put them in their homes

The owner arrives knowing what calls to his heart

He hears the rug in the search for it's

Rightful owner, once viewed the journey begins

If each is a gateway to other times

Then the Tabriz are timeless

They have been, they will be, they are

Tender transformers that

Help soul to remember why it is here.

Historical capital of Iran, Tabriz is considered a summer resort. It was named World Carpet Weaving City in 2015. The population is overwhelmingly Azerbaijani. Tabriz is a major heavy industries hub for automobiles, machine tools, refineries, petrochemicals, textiles, and cement production industries. Very famous for its handicrafts, including hand-woven rugs and jewelry. Tabriz is a site for some of the most prestigious cultural institutes in Northwest Iran. . The Grand Bazaar is one of the best known in rug world.

Tabriz was at the forefront of Iranian rule over its Caucasian territories. Until 1925 the prince of Qajar lived here. Over history it has belonged to many empires, each adding its unique flavor! Most Iranian rugs are labeled by the city or village where they were woven. Rug identification gets interesting as weavers from different regions marry and share their treasured family patterns.

Soulful Sarouks

Set in sensuous symmetry

Sarouks require sincere sanctity

They are soulfully serious statements

Solitude suits them stupendously

Sarouk carpets are made of shiny wool with a Persian knot on a double warp of cotton, which gives a strong and durable carpet. Carpets in red and blue colors are common, sometimes with stylized floral motifs. Sarouk rugs have been produced for much of the twentieth century.

The early successes of the Sarouk rug are largely owed to the American market. From the 1910s to 1950s, the "American Sarouk", also known as the "painted Sarouk", was produced. American customers had an affinity for the Sarouk's curvilinear and floral designs. What they did not appreciate, however, was the color, so for much of the 1920s, 1930s and 1940s, rugs exported from Iran were dyed to a desirable, deep, raspberry-red color, once they arrive in the USA. In the second half of the 19th century, a huge market was created in Europe for Persian rugs. Merchants exported them to other countries. Tabriz was where they shipped them to Turkey, and then from there to Europe and North America.

Isfahan

These exquisite creations are wool and silk on super fine silk foundations. Rugs from Isfahan have very recognizable patterns.

Isfahan creates fine quality rugs due to the influence of supervised weaving production by master weavers called Usta. In the 1920s, between two world wars, was weaving again taken seriously by the people of Isfahan. They started to weave Safavid designs and once again became one of the most important nexuses of the Iranian rug weaving industry. Isfahan carpets today are among the most wanted in world markets, having many customers in western countries. Isfahan rugs and carpets usually have ivory backgrounds with blue, rose, and indigo motifs. Isfahan rugs and carpets often have very symmetrical and balanced designs. Their designs are usually are a medallion that is surrounded with vines and palmettos.

The most famous master weaver in Isfahan is Sarafian. Some years back, when I first started writing about rugs, I wrote this poem about rugs from Isfahan. It was published in PEYK the Persian / English Magazine in 2008.

Eye catching Isfahan

The eye-catching Isfahan's

Lure me into the story

I await here with poems for you

I await here in silken rapture

Admire my colors

Acknowledge my quality

Accept my expression of beauty

See my mysteries waiting for attention

Each color a divine secret.

A great rug will "talk" to you. Most hand-made woven piece of art sometimes taking hundreds of hours to make that is often endowed with the creative insight of the weavers and the skill of the dyers. There is so much love and passion in these items they literally speak volumes. I have always felt that these woven articles almost call out to the buyer. A certain pattern, color or region will make the client almost ecstatic. This what I consider "when a rug speaks". I have been known to get pretty excited about this subject in general.

Solitude

The solitude

Between the wool and the silk

The rugs whisper to me

"Learn my legend please"

That someone may know and share their grandeur

Vivid violet, cream the color of newborn goats

Richly robust hues

The fibers and the colors holding secrets

That shared solitude keeps.

Hamadan

The rugs of the Hamadan Region are only now being recognized for their rightful place in Persian rugs as there are so many areas in Hamadan it is more like a country than a region. 1500 distinct rug weaving villages in Hamadan each of which produced at least two styles of rug. One of the reasons for the variety is the history of the people of the region. When Hamadan history comes up everyone seems to want to start back in the days of Ecbatana and Queen Esther (Hadassah) and her uncle Mordechai. In the 1720s, Nadir Shah pushed the Turks out of the Hamadan region.

With the Persian victory many of the Sunni tribes and villagers retreated to Turkish controlled lands. The majority of Hamadan rugs have a geometric pattern.

Designs consist of medallion-and-corner, and all-over boteh or Herati.

Diamond and hexagon medallions are common. Often the all-over Herati designs have a narrow field in the shape of a large octagon creating corners. There are many variations each with its own unique flavor.

Happy Hamedan's

Having Happy Hamedan's

Happens quite harmoniously

How they hear your heart!

Heavenly healing your fears!

Tangible Language

There is a story behind and woven in every rug.

The weavers speak in fiber and in color, a tangible language.

Their story intertwined with the story of their people and the history of their land. As we connect to the beauty of their story, the people come to life.

For many generations the symbols of everyday life became a language that was elevated to an art.

Revealing the beauty of their inner selves, a sense of tradition from repetition. Their strength, their power is from the continuous strand that touches heaven to earth.

Many weaving cultures have myths and legends about the origin of weaving. Textiles have also been associated in several cultures with the spinning of spiders. Invented in the 14th century, the spindle has a special place in many cultures.

"In those places which were formerly feared, where a man fears... to go on the road, in my days even women walked with spindles" the goddess of weaving, Neath, was a mighty aid in war as well. She protected the Red Crown of Lower Egypt before the two kingdoms were merged, and in Dynastic times she was known as the most ancient one, to whom the other gods went for wisdom. Nit is identifiable by her emblems: most often it is the loom's shuttle, with its two recognizable hooks at each end, upon her head. In Greece the three fates, as stated in my title poem weave the yarns of our destiny. They control it by spinning the thread of life on the distaff. The wife of the god Dionysius in Minoan Crete had possessed the spun thread that led Theseus to the labyrinth center and safely out. The Olympians say that Athena is the goddess of weaving. In that legend, the Odyssey, the craft of weaving is given divine stature. It is an example of work ethic, discipline, and attention to detail.

In Roman literature, Philomena uses her loom becomes her voice, and the story is told in the design. The understanding in the Philomena myth that pattern and design convey myth and ritual has been of great use to modern Mythographers. Growing up, the grandmother that taught us how to sew, had a sister Philomena back in Poland. I love how threads of my life fit in the threads of my story. In Norse literature, Frigg is the goddess of weaving. The Scandinavian myth the Valkyries were described as women weaving on a loom, with severed heads for weights, arrows for shuttles, and human gut for the warp, singing an exultant song of carnage. In Germanic mythology, Bertha and Holds were both known as goddesses who oversaw spinning and weaving. They had many names.

In Baltic myth, the life-affirming sun goddess is named Saule whose numinous presence is signed by a wheel or a rosette. She spins the sunbeams. Madame Okolo, in the legends of the Inca, first taught women the art of spinning thread.

The goddess weaver floated down on a shaft of moonlight with her two attendants according to Chinese myths of the Tang Dynasty. She showed the that a goddess's robe is seamless, for it is woven without the use of needle and thread, entirely on the loom. The phrase "a goddess's robe is seamless" passed into an idiom to express perfect workmanship. This idiom is also used to mean a perfect, comprehensive plan.

In a Japanese folklore, one features a weaving theme. A crane, rescued by a childless elderly couple, appears to them in the guise of a girl who cares for them out of gratitude for their kindness and is adopted as their daughter. She secretly begins weaving stunningly beautiful cloth for the couple to sell under the condition that they may not see her weave. Another variation is that a prince marries the crane as she turns into a woman. In more modern tales, the patron saint of tapestry workers is St Francis of Assisi, and St Blaise is known as the patron saint of wool workers and is revered in the Roman Catholic Church.

The weaving of pile rugs is a difficult and tedious process which, depending on the quality and size of the rug, may take anywhere from a few months to several years to complete. To begin making a rug, one needs a foundation consisting of warps: strong, thick threads of cotton, wool or silk which run the length of the rug and wefts similar threads which pass under and over the warps from one side to the other. The warps on either side of the rug are normally combined into one or more cables of varying thickness that are overcast to form the selvedge. Weaving normally begins by passing a few wefts through the bottom warp to form a base to start from. Loosely piled knots of dyed wool or silk are then tied around consecutive sets of adjacent warps to create the intricate patterns in the rug.

As more rows are tied to the foundation, these knots become the pile of the rug. Between each row of knots, one or more shots of weft are passed to tightly pack down and secure the rows. Depending on the fineness of the weave, the quality of the materials and the expertise of the weavers, the knot count of a handmade rug can vary anywhere from 16 to 800 knots per square inch.

When the rug is completed, the warp ends form the fringes that may be weft-faced, braided, tasseled, or secured in some other manner.

Two basic knots are used in Turkish or Ghiordes knot (used in Turkey, the Caucasus, East Turkmenistan, and some Turkish and Kurdish areas of Iran), and the asymmetrical Persian or Senna knot (Iran, India, Turkey, Pakistan, China, and Egypt).In making a Turkish knot, the yarn is passed between two adjacent warps, brought back under one, wrapped around both forming a collar, then pulled through the center so that both ends emerge between the warps.

The Persian knot is used for finer rugs. The yarn is wrapped around only one warp, then passed behind the adjacent warp so that it divides the two ends of the yarn. The Persian knot may open on the left or the right, and rugs woven with this knot are generally more accurate and symmetrical. Other knots include the Spanish knot looped around single alternate warps, so the ends are brought out on either side and the Jufti knot which is tied around four warps instead.

Kashan, the home of Kashan Rugs is an oasis town on the old north/south caravan route along the west edge of the Dasht-e Kavir desert. These carpets and rugs have the greatest popularity among carpets from Iran.

They all have similar patterns--a single medallion in the center and Persian floral motifs, including arabesques and flower-stems, palmettos, rosettes, blossom, and leaf motifs, forming one of the densest patterns. Kashan rugs and carpets are one of the finest looking carpets on the market. Colors typically are Ivory, light green and red predominate.

Other colors such as soft green and blue are found in newer carpets. I used to explain if family from overseas was bringing you a rug, most likely it would be a Kashan.

Kashan rugs and carpets have soft wool and a thin, tight pile and are woven with the Persian knot. Safavid-period Kashan carpets were often silk, with gold and silver threads woven into the designs. The Kashan's from the early 1900's was typically silk. We had a few of these pieces, luxurious silk in pale blue and creams, so exquisite! Animal scenes and gardens were popular themes. Once there was a rug a customer brought in for a cleaning and it was bought from the owner's father In Tabriz, many decades before! This is the part of rug world I love so much, the stories that each piece has!

In the later period, warp and weft were usually cotton. Double wefts create an effect of depressed knots. In the older days 100% silk Kashan rugs were common. Now the pile is typically wool. Kashan carpets generally have a high knot count. Prayer carpets were popular during the later period, as were pictorial carpets. Manchester wool from Britain, also called Merino wool, which is very fine was used in the late nineteenth and first quarter of the twentieth century in Kashan carpets. At the onset of the Great Depression, weavers switched to local wools and this created a difference. The exquisite quality of Manchester wool allowed a higher knot count and well-executed, crisp motifs in a lustrous carpet with a high pile. The finest quality of Kashan carpets are called Makhteshim. Cecil Edwards, representative of the Oriental Carpet Manufacturers in the early 1900's, attributed them to Haj Mullah Hassan, a merchant in the wool trade in the 1890's who married a woman from Arak.

The story says his wife is said to have used the Manchester wool to make carpets with characteristics of the Sarouk style and a knot count often between 200 and 400 knots per square inch. Tulip and blossom borders that are found on many Makhteshim carpets resemble older Arak rugs, as does the use of lavender in the selvage. Some carpets are signed as Makhteshim adding credence to the idea that they were from a single workshop.

The Secret of the Rugs

Lost between sentences.

Silent innuendos in the conversation as the

gift to communicate is misunderstood by untrained ears.

You must listen close and be patient as

the secret of the rugs is not revealed quickly

One must have focus, so many calling out when you

Arrive it is a calm and stable heart that hears best.

Ardabil are colorful tribal rugs. Some rugs tend to look like Persian copies of Caucasian designs. The reason for this is that when the Russians expanded into the Caucasus in the day of the Christian Czars many Shia Moslems moved out of the newly Russian areas and into present day Iran. Our favorite choices are for runners from this area.

The best examples of rugs from Ardabil are a famous pair. One is at the Victoria and Albert Museum, the other at the LA Art Museum. As I type this, I realize what a divine connection of sorts! In 1998 I worked at the Museum of Fine Arts in Houston, for a traveling show of the Victoria and Albert Museum. I have been to the LA County Art Museum with a family friend that had an antique and rug business in Old Orchard, Maine and then Corona del Mar. I have felt there must be some inner knowing on my part!

The carpets are typical Tabriz work, with one central medallion and smaller, ornate designs surrounding. Such medallions and shapes were central to the design and reality of Persian gardens, a common symbol of paradise for an Islam follower. Completed during the mid-16th century, the carpets are considered some of the best of the classical Iranian (Persian) school of carpet creation. They were installed in a Mosque in Ardabil. Another strange coincidence, one of the first rugs I ever did some color restoration on was originally from a Mosque and the traffic pattern was worn to the warp and weft. They were sold in 1890 carpet broker who was British as they were very worn. He restored one of the carpets using the other and then resold the restored one to the Victoria and Albert Museum, famous architect William Morris suggested to the V&A in the acquisition. They have a poem from Hafiz, a Persian mystic poet;

I have no refuge in the world other than thy threshold.

There is no protection for my head other than this door.

The work of the servant of the threshold Maqsud of Kashan in the year 946.

The carpet was sold by the dealer Edward Stebbing of Richardson and Company as "The Holy Carpet of the Mosque at Ardebil", stressing the "exceptionalism of the carpet and its provenance. He recognized it as a product of the Safavid royal atelier of Shah Tahmasp, made for the Safavid dynastic shrine at Ardabil. Morris wrote in a letter that there was only one, later they realized it was a pair.

When the Victoria and Albert Museum began to check out the piece in 1914, the historical consensus came to be that the modifications on the current Los Angeles Ardabil to repair the London Ardabil were managed by Ziegler and Company, the first buyer of the carpets from Persian resident Hildebrand Stevens, supposedly using Tabriz or Turkish craftsmen. The second Ardabil had visible changes in its structure, as seen in the LACMA image, with its borders replaced into a newly woven narrow line while the London Ardabil was thoroughly over-restored. Historians of the time spoke to this, stating 'The highest market value was for complete carpets, rather than damaged ones or fragments. The London carpet was 'a remarkable work of Art', and as Morris has said, of real historical importance, but it had been compromised to suit the market values of 19th century art connoisseurship.' The carpet was for decades displayed hanging on a wall. Since 2006, it has been shown flat in a special glass pavilion in the center of the Jameel gallery, the lighting is kept low to prevent fading.

The second "secret" carpet, smaller, made up from the remaining usable sections, was sold to the American businessmen Mackay, then to client named Yerkes, and De la Mare art collections, it was eventually revealed and shown in 1931in London at an exhibition. An American industrialist,whom is the well-known, J .Paul Getty, bought it from Lord Duveen for approximately $70,000 several years later. Getty was approached by agents on who offered $250,000 to give to King Farouk of Egypt, so that it could be given as a wedding present for his sister and the Shah of Iran. Getty later donated the carpet to the Los Angeles County Museum of Science, History, and Art. Other fragments have appeared on the market from time to time. The knot density is higher on the Los Angeles carpet. It now resides in the Los Angeles County Museum of Art in Los Angeles.

Majestic Mahals

In a time of regal splendor
A colorful carpet was brought to life
Warmly wonderful woven wools
Reds and captivating creams
Portraying a perfect portrait of proportion
Majestic Mahals mirror the soul

So many years in the Rug Gallery, beyond time and space.

Heriz rugs are from the area of East Azerbaijan in northwest Iran, northeast of Tabriz. Such rugs are produced in the village of the same name in the slopes of Mount Sabalan. Heriz carpets are extremely durable and hard-wearing and they can last for generations. Such rugs age well and become more and more beautiful with age. Part of the reason for the toughness of Heriz carpets is that Mount Sablan sits on a major deposit of copper. Traces of copper in the drinking water of sheep produces high quality wool that is far more resilient than wool from other areas. Heriz rug weavers often make them in geometric, bold patterns with a large medallion dominating the field. Such designs are traditional and often woven from memory.

Hear the Happy Heriz

Look into your heart

You will hear the happy Heriz!

Filling your world with light and color.

Patterns so geometric and true!

Like the mixing of cultures by a divine chemist.

Their history fascinated me,

Calling for my attention.

Forever grateful I will be that I took

The time to listen to the mirth

Of the happy Heriz.

Heartfelt Herati

A brightly colored

Complex creation

Invites one to look closer

Examine every exquisite emblem

That when woven as one

Brings wonder

The symmetry of symbols

Frolicking fishes of the sea

Delightful daisies

As if on a summer day

Fresh picked enfolded before you

Heratis are a heartfelt hybrid

Of high style, delightful discipline

From town to town

The explicit beauty is

Admired and copied.

Bijar rugs, known as the Iron Rugs of Iran, are mostly considered village rugs because whether woven in the town of Bijar itself or its surrounding villages, they are woven inside houses rather than workshops. The pattern of Bijar rugs is a combination of curvilinear and geometric with curvilinear being dominant. The favorite colors of Bijar weavers consist of navy, cherry red, brown, light blue, pink, yellow, ocher, orange, beige, and ivory. The symmetrical (Turkish) knot is mainly used although the asymmetrical (Persian) knot is seen as well. The most typical pattern, the Herati motif, is a repeated field design which normally consists of a flower centered within a diamond surrounded by curved leaves parallel to each side of the diamond. This can be in various forms in either geometric or curvilinear designs.

Beautiful Bijars

Behold Beautiful Bijars!
Bold, bodacious colors.
Strong like iron, their value and inner light.
Are revealed when they are little worn.
Washed and Cleaned.
They will last a hundred of years.
Just like happiness, beautiful Bijars.

CHAPTER 16

PAKISTAN

The manufacturing of Pakistani carpets began in the same way as in India and when the country was separated from India most of the weavers moved to the Pakistan side. Most of them found jobs in Lahore and Karachi, and at the same time the government began to support the import of quality yarn. Pakistani rugs are manufactured nowadays with fine Australian wool yarn making these rugs very similar to silk carpets. Pakistani carpets with a high knot density provide strong durability at a lower price than its Persian parallels. Most are created with vegetable dyes and have a very pleasing organic feel.

Pakistani rugs are normally described by the actual number of knots vertically and horizontally "16/16" or "16/18" which would equal 288 knots per square inch (16 x 18). These are called "double knot" where the shape of the knots makes it look like there are two knots rather than one. The typical styles are: The most popular styles are Bohkaras, Chobi, Ziegler, Pakistani Persian (Pak Persian), Bokhara, Jaldar, Kazak, Heriz, Beljik (made with Belgian fine wool) and Gabbeh. The art of weaving rugs in Pakistan began in the ancient Indus Valley civilization. In Moenjo-Daro and Harappa found signs of early weavers through spindles and other weaving materials. Lahore and Karachi are where these weavers settled. During the Shah Jahan's reign, the Pakistani way of weaving entered its golden age. The news about these rug carpets spread and the demand for it reached the whole of South Asia and abroad. Nowadays the government supports the importation of quality yarn and make use of Australian and New Zealand wool. Hand-knotted rugs is the second-largest industry in Pakistan.

The rugs from Pakistan I am most familiar with is the Chobi type of rug. Chobi rugs are also known as Ghazni or Peshawar rugs. With higher-knot density and top-notch quality makes them very long lasting.

Peshawar carpet rugs come from Northwestern Pakistan, where many Afghan weavers migrated and settled over the years. These are hand-knotted pieces of fine rugs dyed using natural sources. What makes Peshawar rugs very different is that the use simple designs, letting each pattern stand out. They are dyed primarily with vegetable dyes and their color palette makes them very attractive. Jaldar rugs came from the traditional Pakistani Sarouk and Yamud designs. They are made with diamond-shaped motifs aligned in rows and they are made with the Ghiordes knot. The Pakistani carpets at this time are made in Lahore, Karachi and Rawalpind. They are classified as either Mori carpets or Persian where 90% of the Mori carpets have a Bochara-like pattern and other Turkmenistan patterns. The other styles of carpets, that are manufactured in Pakistan, have patterns that are copied from older Persian traditions in the Arak district, such as the favorites like Chobis (based on Zeigler patterns) and the geometric Kazaks.

Pensive Pakistanis

Colors so Precise

They are different in the story

Of life they depict

Bright new materials

Showing wisdom greater than their age

They call out quietly to me

Expressing their own style

Delighting us daily!

Baluchi beauties

To me the most incredibly beautiful tribal rugs are from Baluchistan. One reason is that Baluchistan crosses three borders: Iran, Pakistan, Afghanistan Most Baloch nomads live in Pakistan some live closer to India. The type began as prayer rugs.

The materials that make up these rugs are made of are cotton, wool, and camel hair. Most piles are made of wool and camel hair, occasionally silk is added. In all the variations the predominant colors are red, black, cream. Antique one will have blues, brown and purple. Repeating patterns are symbols like hexagons, rectangles, and triangles. Since most weavers are nomadic, the smaller sizes are in abundance.

The population is mainly in two groups. Sulaimani and the Makrani and have been around since the 10th century. The Sulaimans is composed of a few tribes which consists of a few clans. Baloch nomads raise camels, sheep and goats and engage in carpet making and embroidery.

The main ethnic groups in the province are the Baloch people and the Pashtuns, who constitute 52% and 36% of the population respectively (according to the preliminary 2011 census). The remaining 12% comprises smaller communities of Brahuis, Hazaras along with other settlers such as Sindhis, Punjabis, Uzbeks and Turkmens. The name "Baluchistan" means "the land of the Baloch". Largely underdeveloped, its provincial economy is dominated by natural resources, especially its natural gas fields, estimated to have sufficient capacity to supply Pakistan's demands over the medium to long term. Baluchistan occupies the very southeastern-most portion of the Iranian Plateau, the setting for the earliest known farming settlements in the pre-Indus Valley Civilization era, the earliest of which was Mehrgarh, dated at 7000 BC, within the province. Baluchistan marked the westernmost extent of the Civilizations. Centuries before the arrival of

Islam in the 7th Century, parts of Baluchistan was ruled by the Paratarajas, an Indo-Scythian dynasty. Baloch people, believe that they are of Median descent.

The beauty of these rugs reflects the nomadic spirit of the weavers. You will see color and pattern differences depending on the ethnicity of your weaver.

CHAPTER 17

INDIAN RUGS

Incredible Indians

Millions and Billions of Carpets!

Intriguing designs!

Innovative colors!

Created with a precision only known

To those with thousands of years of history

With one thread in the ancient past

And the rest the fibers of the future.

How a country of such contrasts

Weaves such wonders

Is incredible!

Indian weaving began in the 16th century when the Great Mughal Akbar took over the reign in India. He loved beautiful objects much like his grandfather, Babur, who had been a long time in Persia. Wanting to add some glamour to the palace, Akbar brought to Agra, the capital, a few best carpet weavers from Persia. Persian craftsmen were able to start the weaving industry in India practically from scratch. Local workshops were created in Agra, Delhi, and Lahore. 1520-1530 Akbar established weaving trainings to teach the prisoners of Agra jails. The inmates became artisans. Those created are named of Jail Indian Rugs or Prison Indian Rugs.

Akbar's innovations earned him a nearly divine status with his Moghul empire. Then over time their motifs became softer and sophisticated. Indian attention for detail, combined with original patterns and excellent quality, gained world-wide recognition. Then the industry seemed to decline in quality with only the finest rugs being made in Srinagar, Amritsar, and Agra. In the 19th century Indian Rugs Amritsar rugs came into being and were completely different from the rest, Amritsar rugs are based upon European influence and Western taste carpets in both the United States and Europe during the nineteenth century. The weavers of Amritsar weavers used high quality wool, Amritsar rugs are manufactured with a cotton foundation, double weft, and an asymmetrical knot - all of which contribute to its luxurious feel. Indian cities have amazing gardens, and these rugs give both owners and appreciators of these rugs a feeling like they are immersed in a garden. We see roses, carnations, lilies, and Henna blossoms of the rug woven in pale blues, yellows, teals, eggplants, and burgundies. With India's restoration of independence in 1947, the manufacturing of Indian carpets has slowly begun to recover. Most of the weavers moved to Pakistan, India managed to educate a lot of new artisans. Under the program, large groups of women have been trained, what allowed the renewal of the market. Modern day weaving of rugs in India are most well-known are Kashmir, Jaipur, Agra and Bhadohi. Rugs from Kashmir are predominantly silk, Jaipur dense and durable floral wools, Agra has some super fine wools comparable to Persian quality, and Bhadohi hosts much of the modern style of rug manufacturing. In fact, back in 2014 I was invited to attend the yearly carpet show in Bhadohi. It seemed like an intriguing idea, and perhaps one day I will attend!

There are so many things I love about rugs! The weaving is totally unique to region and that has so much to do with which type of wool is available. Before we go there, I will share a little bit of some of the rugs you may not know about! Let's for fun look at the types of creatures that we get our wool from!

Inside my Tapestry

A complex woven story: The tapestry of my life

Came to light this morning.

Why was I drawn into the rugs?

I was in a state of spiritual excitation.

The world of mere mortals pained me.

Contemplating the mysteries of the spiritual worlds occupied my mind and spirit for many years.

The wonders of rugs gave me a place to go to be peaceful in my soul.

Years of adventures and being in danger, made the solitude of fibers a welcoming embrace.

The patterns intrigued me beyond belief! Understanding they had a story deep within.

They might depict familiar facets of the weaver's life.

They may be. A cultural symbol of power.

Religious symbolism is prominent. What weavers believe is that rugs provide the owner. With protection.

Inside my tapestry I feel safe.

CHAPTER 18

WEAVING THE AMERICAS

Did you know there are rugs made in South America?

When you look up rugs from Brazil, the most popular item is their cowhide rugs! This is modern Brazil at its best, tasteful if that type of rug is for you. So, what about the history of weaving there? Currently it's a hub of weaving synthetics and a power in the leather industry. To look at weaving its best to consider the whole of South America as in earlier times borders were more invisible.

"It is believed that the Americas were settled by three migratory waves from Northern Asia. The Native Brazilians are thought to descend from the first wave of migrants, who arrived in the region around 9000 BC. The main Native Brazilian groups are the Caribs, the Je, the Tupi-Guarani, and the Arawak's. As I write this story, I am astounded how my own story is woven in. My first plane ride was with my family in 1972 to Rio de Janeiro via Caracas, Venezuela. We stayed in an old part of town which was very much colonial Portuguese. We visited a family friend that showed us some of the art districts near the favelas. For sure it left a deep impression for me. I have sold rugs to people from everywhere, including Brazil. One holiday time, as I write this version in December, I met a rug collector from there and his family. That's what I love best how my love of rugs ties me to others who feel the same.

The European to Brazil migration was primarily from Portugal. In the first two centuries of colonization, 100,000 Portuguese arrived in Brazil (around 500 colonists per year). In the 18th century, 600,000 Portuguese arrived (6,000 per year). The Cablecos group have always been present in many parts of Brazil. Another important ethnic group, Africans, first arrived from mainly West African countries, as slaves.

The end of the eighteenth century many had been taken from the Congo, what is now Nigeria, Angola, immigrants to Brazil occurred in the late 19th and early 20th centuries. Brazil attracted nearly 5 million immigrants around 1870. These immigrants were divided in two groups: a part of them was sent to work as small farmers in Southern Brazil. The biggest part of the immigrants was sent to the coffee plantations in the Southeast. Here I also feel a thread, my maternal grandmother, Emilia (Boltruczyk) Kosciuczyk when she emigrated from Poland, went to cousins in Western Massachusetts to help on the tobacco farm. This fact I didn't know until later in life.

My aunt told us stories about the family as adults. All of them have left the earth, and I feel grateful that in the way the stories were shared to me much the way weaving is shared in the generations. In fact, this grandmother taught me how to sew and sing songs in Polish. Weavers are known to sing a song to direct the weaving.

The immigrants sent to Brazil were from Germany, Italy, Portugal and Spain, especially Andalusia. Notably, the first half of the 20th century saw a large inflow of Japanese and folks from Lebanon and Syria and are called Turks because of their rulers at that time. A few years back I was seeing where any family might be in the world, and there was quite a branch of Kosciuczyk in South America. Many folks from eastern Europe moved there during World War II.

I walked into a house and there were some handmade rugs from Ecuador. That's right, Ecuador! Completely fascinated they had the most in common with Persian Gabbeh. I do have a book of South American textiles but something about their uniqueness captured my heart. The owner inherited them from her family, and they were from 1940-1950's. Olga Fisch was the designer. She was an artist from 1901-1990. An extraordinary artist as well as an art dealer and cultural expert who was born in Hungary. She was a phenomenal traveler through the jungles of South America and went to live in Morocco. She specialized in cultural handicrafts and made her way by plane, boats even zeppelins and was associated with Quito, Ecuador. The type of Gabbeh she made were about 65,000 knots per square meter. Conquered villages were put to all aspects of weaving. Moving from personal looms to industrial ones really improved their product and process. The tasks were both agricultural and material. They raised sheep, clean and spun yarn, dyeing and weaving fibers and selling their products. Weaving can be time consuming and the industrialization by Spain made it more grueling, but it worked! Workers owned a small plot and worked in the factories. These organized haciendas became role models. This type of feudal system was in place until 1964. For more information visit Otavalo Obraje Museum.

If we think tribal rugs are their own language. One of the most distinctive styles are the rugs of the Navajo Nation. Native American rugs are more of an individual's artistic vision. Their unique factor is that major improvements have been accomplished by a small group of individuals. One change to materials and/or distribution has resulted in whole new styles and much innovation.

There is much to be said about Navajo rugs. When caring for these items think of them more as finely woven tapestries. Nathan Koets, a fellow rug lover, is an expert and is glad to share his advice about their care. The Navajo Nation known as the Dineh in their language are Athabascan-speaking people who migrated to the Southwest from Canada in about the 15th century. Navajo women learned weaving in the mid-1600s from their Pueblo Indian neighbors who had been growing and weaving cotton since about 800 AD. When the Spanish settlers had brought their Churro sheep to the region in the early 1600s and introduced the Navajo to wool. They were well known among both their Indian and Spanish neighbors for finely woven, nearly weatherproof blankets that became popular trade items. Garments-especially wearing blankets-comprised most of the products of early Navajo looms and were wider than long (when the warp was held vertically) and were known as mantas. Many people appreciated Navajo weaving, especially those of the Arts & Crafts design movement found that the bold designs complimented with their simple furniture and handmade accessories.

In 1896, C.N. Cotton, a trader in Gallup, New Mexico had issued a catalog to expand his market to eastern retailers. Lorenzo Hubble at Ganado, Arizona and J.B. Moore at Crystal, New Mexico, followed up with their own catalogs in the early years of the new century, focusing specifically on rugs. Navajo weaving had quickly gained a national audience.

Juan Lorenzo Hubbell was the leading trader of the early period in rug-making and owned several trading posts around the Reservation with his home and base at Ganado, Arizona about 50 miles south of Canyon de Chelly. Weavers worked as well at trading post at Klagetoh, Arizona (also owned by Hubbell). They often worked in the same colors and patterns but reversed the color scheme and used a grey ground with red, white, and black central motifs. The Ganado and Klagetoh style rugs continue to be most popular of all Navajo rug designs. Others we will explore are Crystal, storm pattern, Two grey hills, Shiprock, tree of life with corn, Yeibichai (gods), sand painting styles, and saddle style.

Chief's Blanket is a specific style with the First Phase blankets were made from about 1800 to 1850. They consisted simply of brown (or blue) and white stripes with the top, bottom and center stripes usually being wider than the others. Second Phase blankets included small red rectangles at the center and ends of the darker stripes and were made about 1840 to 1870.

The Third Phase type, between 1860 and 1880, saw the addition of stepped or serrated diamonds of color to the center and ends of the wide stripes.

The Fourth Phase, made from 1870 through the early 1900s, diamond motifs became larger and more elaborate, often overtaking the stripes as primary design elements. In my years of working with rugs, mostly Persian, I occasionally had some Navajo Rugs to appraise or on consignment. I did have a granddaughter of a weaver bring some rugs for sale and I was happy to put her in contact with the collector.

Originally most known weaving in the tribes was primarily for blankets for personal use. Some of the initial traders that brought this art to the mainstream: Juan Lorenzo Hubbell from the post in Ganado, Arizona, and John. B. Moore ran the post at Crystal, New Mexico. Some other notable names in the field are L.C.' Cozy 'Mc Sparron and the renowned Mary Cabot Wheelwright from Boston who created the Museum of Navajo Ceremonial Art.

As in fine artistry some names have more talent and work associated with them, when looking into specific Individual weavers. Of note are Daisy Taugelchee from Two Grey Hills and Margaret Begay from Wide Ruins. Some locations were associated with fine quality weavings such as the Bosque Redondo, and Ganado Post. To this day if your weaver was from one of these clans you can be sure of the authenticity of your art, Other influences of note were the inclusion of Navajo designs in Pendleton's Blankets. They sent their textile designer to live with the Indians to learn their color and design preferences, thus creating one of the first Navajo inspired lines of products. Recently while working in flooring, I met a client in her 90's who was looking for a rug of practical material to compliment her Navajo Antique rugs. I asked her which designs and to my amazement when I said Two Grey Hills, her eyes lit up. Suddenly I made a new friend again because of woven rugs! I knew what colors to show her, and I delivered them and was privileged to see her collection of antique rugs.

CHAPTER 19

WEAVING IN ISRAEL

The Old Testament makes frequent mention of the weaving of textiles. So, I also talked with an Intellectual Property Attorney who shared me the photo of the rug he bought in Israel. Israel? I realized I hadn't explored that topic yet. I work in flooring and carpeting and there are some lines that are made there. Until this moment I had not read much. So here are some facts I found.

The Bible also talks about dyes such as Kermes, and I also had visited a site where they dyed "Tyre Purple" in Rhodes, Greece during biblical times. It was from a shell found in the Mediterranean Sea and chief city of ancient Phoenicia, now stands the town of Sur in southern Lebanon. The Bible talks about dyeing the tabernacle textiles in the book of Exodus. The reddish-purple wool was dyed with mollusks (Murex truncus's and Murex brandaris). There is a gland containing a drop of creamy white fluid. When exposed to air and light it gradually becomes reddish purple to deep violet. Tyrian purple as this type of dye is called, is a photosensitive type of dye. Its color is determined by the amount of sunlight exposure. Thus "reddish purple " not purple or violet or red but, reddish purple.

Jewish imagery and pieces were woven for synagogue mainly in ancient times. All the way from Egypt to the border of China where we found Jewish communities, we can find ties and links to the rug trade. What most people do not know is that in the twentieth-century pile carpets were woven in present day Israel. Carmel Floor Design' has been the leading Israeli rug and carpet manufacturer in woven and tufted machine-made carpets for over 50 years. The company has an excellent reputation in the production and export of high-quality products, proficient customer service, and affordable prices. In 1903 the Bezalel School of Arts and Crafts was established in Ottoman Jerusalem by Professor Boris Schatz with the help of Theodor Herzl.

Bezalel and Bezalel carpets were a key part of preparing the way for what grew into the Nation-State of Israel. When a weaver expresses his Jewishness in art. Instead of working in a foreign place with foreign peoples whose inner life he cannot understand, he comes back to his homeland, to his own people, whose life is the very soul of himself. Bezalel has become a valuable commercial institution of Palestine by giving employment to hundreds in its rug-weaving, basket making, and filigree workshops

CHAPTER 20

GREECE

What I would like to share with you is my very first rug cleaning experience. When living in Greece floors were marble, and rugs were put on them during winter. Roofs were typically cement and flat and we would in the end of spring wash them with the hose and some soap. Leave on the roof to dry. Simple. The most memorable version was going with friends outside of Corinth for a "Rug Washing Experience". We filled the trunk and roof with Wool flokatis, the car with four people and drove down the dusty roads. We stopped at the Cheese factory to pick up some fresh feta cheese! See the goats and sheep and drive up the twisting roads to Kleitoria. There was a small shack the housed the local "carpet cleaner".

Mountain water coursed through the stream in the middle of the house at a rapid pace. They had built a makeshift bucket in the stream. We would heave the wool fleece rugs in there and there was more than enough water to open the strands and clean the deep-seated dirt. Sometimes a touch of natural made soap was added and stirred with a wooden branch. It would take three of us to carry the wet rug out to the porch where thick stump railings let them dry naturally. Once the rugs were out to dry, we would drive a bit down the road. The stream from up in the mountains had two forks. One went to the cleaners the other to a trout farm. The farm had a restaurant where we would have a nice meal. Eventually we would go back to pick them up. The stream once it cleaned the rugs, powered an old-fashioned grinding stone. We would purchase some of the fresh ground corn and wheat to bake bread. We would wrestle the wet rugs that almost weighed like full sheep onto the roof and the trunk and drive back to the village of Galataki. Our friend's farmhouse had a large flat cement roof. We would spread them out to dry in the hot Greek sun. We would drive back to Athens. Two weeks later perfectly white and clean flokatis!

Flokati is a pure wool rug made in Greece by a unique age-old process. For centuries, Greek rug makers have woven Flokati rugs. They were cherished as family treasures, part of brides' dowries and used as wall-hangings and bed covers as well as rugs. Kleitoria is a village and a municipal unit in Achaea, Peloponnese, Greece. It was also the new name of the former municipality Lefkasio, of which it was the seat, between 2008 and 2011. Once a thriving city with over 60,000 people and one of the first to be established. What is now left of Klitoras now are parts of walls, a theatre, and a few buildings from Hellenistic and Roman times.

CHAPTER 21

CLEANING

Since I worked about 20 years in rugs and flooring, one question often asked is about cleaning. Cleaning your rug is that common sense should prevail: if a rug is badly stained, damaged, or dirtied, if it has been peed on a lot by your pet, if the colors have faded, run, or bled into each other or there are gaping holes where rug used to be, spend the money and have it cleaned and/or repaired professionally - you won't regret it. Same goes for antique, old, or silk and delicate rugs.

Cleansing the Soul

Like a rug to be washed, carefully by hand.

I arrived at the Lords of Karma asking for forgiveness.

Begging for the stains on my soul to be lifted.

The terrors of the past dark shadow nearly blocked all the light from within. So as a carpet is washed, so might my soul be cleaned.

Once the dirt is lifted, the beauty underneath shines.

Bright clean and repaired it becomes the work of art it was destined to be.

No longer damaged it's admired not scorned.

I have tried numerous ways to get involved in rugs. I had managed the 4th Avenue Rug Gallery for 15 years, making friends and connections worldwide and slowly getting involved in social media. I started going to Technology coffee groups and 1million cups entrepreneur events. I got help from other serial entrepreneurs, and a big thanks you go out to those circles, especially Nate Evanich. I tried the "Rug Goddess', Alley Cat Rugs, Cynthia of the Rugs. Always trying new ways to present the material. So many people call me and ask for my advice it spawned two business ideas: Designertastes and a project with a friend in the business called Rugology World ™.

Before and After

Last week the paths converged, and I would never be the same.

I was the grateful recipient of knowledge,

Wealth of prizes, gifts of the spiritual worlds.

These words of wisdom are given to me freely and often.

Speaking with the professors and the philosophers, only confirmed my thoughts.

There is so much more to learn!

Having enlightenment can be at times painful, as it sets you apart from others.

Love being the most important lesson, without love we are nothing.

CHAPTER 22

REPAIRS

A lot of what goes on in the world of rugs is repairs. I always likened it to the work of the Alchemists, in turn the metals to gold they transformed themselves in the process. now.

Maybe there's unraveling or the colors have faded with time and you'd like to restore the rug to its original condition. Find a local expert! If you have a rug shop, they may do it there or know someone to refer you to!

Repairing extensive damage may require changing the pattern of the rug or taking out part of the design. If you want your rug to continue to look the way it originally did, it's best to get it repaired soon before it reaches a point of no return.

Since fringes are delicate and exposed, it's easy for them to become damaged.

And fringe repairs are generally a lot easier and less expensive than repairs to the main pile. These may involve serging the fringe into the side of the rug or adding replacement fringe. For a particularly fine antique rug, we might pull out part of the pile and wrap stitch around every thread of the warp to make it look like the original rug.

Tear repair usually involves simply putting the warps back and reconstructing that small portion of the rug. Holes can generally be repaired if the material around the hole is still in good condition. Moth damage can generally be repaired if it isn't too severe.

If there are missing patches of threads and colors on your rug, it's probably because of hungry moths. Keep an eye out for future damage if you know your rug is made from a particularly moth-vulnerable material, like wool. There's not much you can do about rot if your rug has water damage. You may still be able to save your rug by cutting out that section of the rug. Your rug will be smaller, but it may be able to last a while longer.

Unraveling the threads

Is it fate or destiny? That directs us.

Can life be summed up?

In the threads of a rug?

How do I know the best fit?

Why was I unable to remove the Darkness in my life for so long?

Like a diamond waiting to be polished,

I await my freedom, like rug

That is cleaned and repaired

As if the door to my soul

Was finally allowed to open

The poems are close to my thoughts and dreams today

All is necessary is to reach out and the words form themselves.

So, few see what I see.

Chapter 23

EPILOGUE

I want to thank you all for coming along with me on my journey. The words of Rumi inspired me to write from the first word that my lips spoke. I would love to share stories about rugs or to help with yours. Let's finish this book with a poem from the master.

In the End

In the end, the mountains of imagination were nothing but a house.
And this grand life of mine was nothing but an excuse.
You've been hearing my story so patiently for a lifetime
Now hear this: it was nothing but a fairy tale.

Mewlana Jalaluddin Rumi

CHAPTER 24

JOURNEY

My journey in writing this book took me on a long and winding road less traveled.

As the part of my story began long ago there are a few memories I would like to share.

The first rug I ever saw at my grandmother's home.

The trips to Turkey

Working LVF textile factory

The moment I read my first Rumi poem

That night when I looked up on the wall and saw the Nain with a weaver's eye.

When I met the poet descendent of Ferdowsi and he liked my poems.

When I shared my poems with people in the industry.

The moment I began my journey to publish back in 2003.

References for book:

https://www.smithsonianmag.com/smart-news/in-ancient-rome-purple-dye-was-made-from-snails-1239931/
https://news.mit.edu/2017/analyzing-language-color-0918
https://www.catalinarug.com/blog/the-meaning-behind-9-popular-oriental-rug-colors/
https://www.nejad.com/consumer/rug-names-and-places.html
A Zionist primer: essays by various writers, Editor Sundel Doniger Publisher Young Judea, 1917'
https://handwovenmagazine.com/the-common-language-of-weavers/

PHOTO Credits

Jason Mikaeli, Richard Inman, Stephen Roberts

Shawn Bagheri, Cynthia Kosciuczyk, Adi Pourfard

Lisa Lazarus, Cathy and Larry Snyder, Bruce Koren

Issa Hoker, Brian Jesperson, Shahid Kwhaja, Arefeh Riahi

Ross Brown, Bruce Greenhaus, Mary LaViolette, Public Domain

RUG EXPERTS

ARTISTIC RUG CARE
cleaning | protection | restoration

316-681-8000 www.artisticrugcare.com

Designer Tastes

"Design the strand that connects it all"

linkedin.com/designertastes

Cynthia Kosciuczyk,
BS, MBA

(858) 717-2607
designertastes@gmail.com

- **Textile Appraisals**
- **Design Consultant**
- **Cleaning and Repairs**
- **Flooring Design**
- **Remodeling**

www.DyeboldAcademy.com (813)320-4000

www.jonquilcarpetcleaning.com 678-367-3775

Rob Decker
Master Textile Cleaner
Journeyman Water Restorer
Woolsafe Fabric Care Specialist

Managing Partner

573-817-2540
www.**MaxCareMark**.com
Cell: 573-818-8094

1218 Clinkscales Rd., Columbia, MO 65202

CARPET CLEANING & REPAIR

**CARPET
CLEANING**
IICRC Certified

RUG RENEW

CLEANING · RESTORATION · REPAIRS

www.RugRenew.com 619-462-1020
San Diego local rug cleaning! Located 20 minutes east of the San Diego Airport & Coronado

About the Author

Cynthia has passion for art, food, and science. Loves intelligent conversation and design. As writer, she identifies as a poet. She believes optimism will triumph and hopes as an entrepreneur to make a difference in the world. I wanted to create a book for: art lovers, rug lovers, designers, poetry people and those with a taste for different cultures.

Member: San Diego Press Club

My Poem: San Diego- Emerald City will be in this year's poetry annual

https://sandiegopoetryannual.com/

Writer: Life by design Magazine, Biz Catalyst 360

Contributing author: Letters to me and Thoughts (Overcoming our Obstacles)

will be in the Secret Millionaire's next book on Greatness

Author: https://www.amazon.com/My-Odyssey-Journal-reflections-Journey/dp/1525503170

https://www.linkedin.com/in/cynthia-kosciuczyk-bs-mba-4462127/

Cynthia Kosciuczyk, MBA

(858) 717-2607

cynthia@salonistasays.com

Facebook: Salonista Cynthia

Twitter: @ Salonistasays

Instagram: Designertastes@gmail.com

www.rugology.world

www.designertastes.com

Printed in the United States
by Baker & Taylor Publisher Services